P9-BBT-553

Cake Art

THE CULINARY INSTITUTE OF AMERICA

DESIGNS AND TECHNIQUES BY CHEFS KATE CAVOTTI AND ALISON MCLOUGHLIN

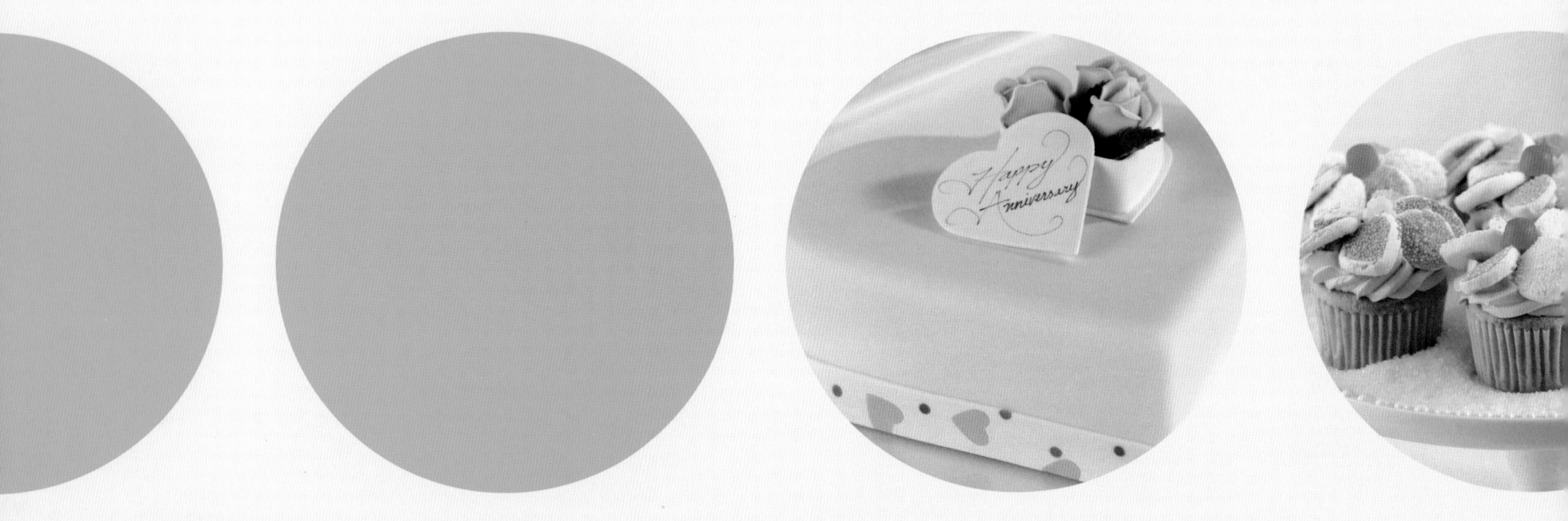

ALSO BY THE CULINARY INSTITUTE OF AMERICA

The Culinary Institute of America's Gourmet Meals in Minutes • *Grilling*

One Dish Meals • *Book of Soups* • *Breakfasts & Brunches* • *Vegetables*

Cake Art

Simplified Step-by-Step Instructions and Illustrated Techniques for the Home Baker to Create Showstopping Cakes and Cupcakes

Text by Lindsay Kincaide
Photography by Diane Padys

LEBHAR-FRIEDMAN BOOKS
NEW YORK • CHICAGO • LOS ANGELES • LONDON • PARIS • TOKYO

THE CULINARY INSTITUTE OF AMERICA

President Dr. Tim Ryan

Vice-President, Continuing Education Mark Erickson

Director of Intellectual Property Nathalie Fischer

Managing Editor Kate McBride

Editorial Project Manager Lisa Lahey

Recipe Testing Manager Maggie Wheeler

Production Assistant Patrick Decker

LEBHAR-FRIEDMAN BOOKS

A company of Lebhar-Friedman, Inc., 425 Park Avenue, New York, New York 10022

Project Manager Maria Tufts

Art Director Kevin Hanek

LIBRARY OF CONGRESS CATALOGING-IN-PUBLICATION DATA

Cataloging-in-publication data for this title is on file with the Library of Congress.

ISBN 0-86730-922-9 | 978-0-86730-922-5

Manufactured in Singapore on acid-free paper

Contents

WE ARE VERY FORTUNATE to be surrounded by so many talented individuals who have helped us to produce this book. Being able to share techniques and our "tricks of the trade" to enthusiastic non-professionals is no easy task.

We would first like to thank our writer, Lindsay Kincaide for painstakingly gathering and putting into words our eclectic thoughts, ideas, recipes, and techniques. This was quite a task with two chefs on different schedules in different places.

A great deal of gratitude goes to photographer Diane Padys and prop stylist Cynthia Verner for their outstanding artistry. Their amazing photography and attention to detail transformed our cakes into works of art. Thank you.

This project would never have succeeded without the support we received from the CIA community. Countless students contributed to this book in different ways; without their efforts we would not have been able to complete the cakes for photography in time. We would especially like to thank Sarah Bozanich, Mary Kathryn Gilday, Bryan Graham, Soojin Kim, Christopher Lucia, Erin McGinn, Suzanne Mulherin, Sean Pera, Lynnsey Ramos, Nelson Salsa, and Deborah Wise. It was their willingness to do whatever it took to get the job done that enabled us to create designs that exceeded our expectations. Their talent and never ending enthusiasm for the project was inspiring. Thank you to our colleagues for encouraging us and sharing their expertise, opinions, and workspace in their kitchens when we had nowhere else to go. Thanks to the carpentry staff for building structural pieces needed for photography and the set.

The team at the Food and Beverage Institute deserves our gratitude for guiding us through the publishing process and keeping us on track. A special thanks to Lisa Lahey, Kate McBride, and Patrick Decker, who were happy to lend their experienced eyes and offer their expertise and encouragement whenever we needed it.

Finally, thank you to our families for dealing with the long hours of production and photography. We worked many hours away from home to make this book a reality, and are grateful to them all for their support and encouragement throughout the whole process.

— CHEF KATE CAVOTTI AND CHEF ALISON MCLOUGHLIN

Cake Decorating 101

THIS BOOK IS as much about creativity as it is about cake decorating. Truly, cake decorating is its own art form, and sugar can be crafted into anything your imagination desires. Cake decorating is a fun activity that can be enjoyed by adults and children of all ages. It provides the opportunity to design and create something of your very own.

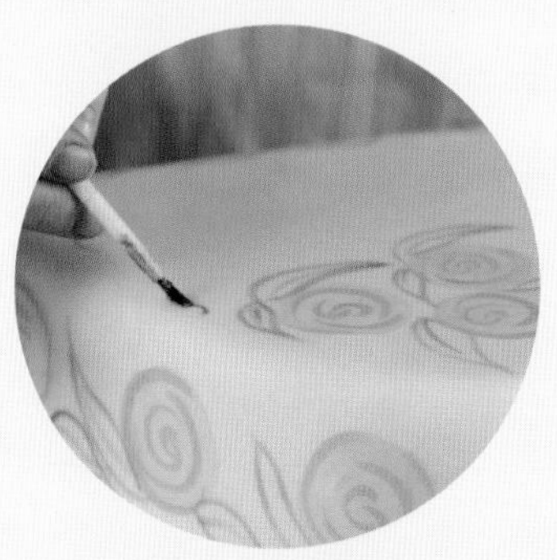

Inspiration for cake themes can come from a variety of sources such as books, photographs, cards, ribbons, toys, and china. Look for interesting patterns or designs on these items that can be recreated with décor mediums. Exploring craft, antique, fabric, and gift stores provides a wealth of inspiration to create an incredible themed cake. You may also find new cake decorating equipment or tools. Designs can be created using rubber stamps and plastic stencils. This book details these techniques and others.

The key to cake decorating is understanding the décor materials and how they can be used with a variety of different techniques. With this knowledge, a piping bag of buttercream can be used to create dozens of designs, and a piece of fondant can be transformed into a lifelike farm animal or a fantasy creature. Similarly, a central theme, such as roses, can be created with different techniques and décor mediums. Delicious roses and other flowers can be piped out of buttercream, meringue, and ganache. For a more realistic flower, modeling chocolate, gum paste, or fondant can be hand shaped into petals to form beautiful roses and buds. In addition, food

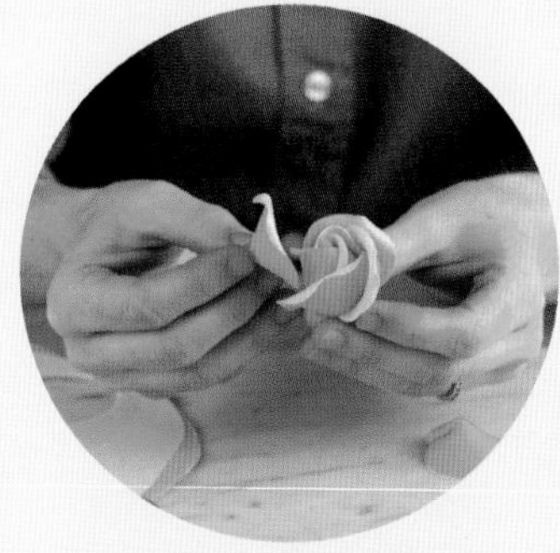

colors or food-color markers can be used to paint or draw roses onto a cake that has been covered in fondant. Using a variety of décor mediums on a cake will create depth and interest.

A cake should be well thought out before decorating begins; but this planning process can be fun, and involving children in the design of a cake will allow them to stretch their creativity. Begin by creating a sketch of the cake that includes the number of tiers and the placement of the decorations. This is the time to think about the type of décor mediums that will be used to both cover the cake and make the décor pieces. You should also consider the dish, plate, or cake stand on which you wish to assemble the cake. This book includes detailed instructions about how to properly bake and assemble a single or multi-tiered cake so that you will have a foundation for your decorations. It is important to remember that a beautiful cake will be admired when presented, but taste is equally important. We have included a chapter with some delicious recipes for cakes and fillings, as well as guidelines on flavor pairings.

The next step is to create the individual decorations that will embellish the cake, most of which can be prepared in advance, and then bake and assemble the cake. Decorative garnishes, such as modeling chocolate roses or gum paste figures, can be made several days in advance and then stored in a dry place until you are ready to decorate. Piping with buttercream, meringue, royal icing, or ganache should be done as close as possible to serving time. When you are ready to decorate, have all of the components laid out neatly, so that you know what you have to work with. It is especially important to be well prepared when decorating with children, because they are usually very excited to get started!

The final, and undoubtedly most fun, stage is the decorating itself. Certain décor

OPPOSITE: *Inspiration can be found all around us, from a wide variety of materials.*

BELOW, LEFT: *Once inspired, create a sketch of the cake that includes size, placement of the decorations, serving dish, and how the cake will be iced.* **CENTER:** *Assemble the cake and create the individual decorations; have other décor tools ready, such as piping bags of icing.* **RIGHT:** *The finished product will no doubt greatly resemble your sketch, but don't hesitate to make changes along the way.*

happy birthday xxx

sprinkles
sprinkles

may need to be secured to the cake with royal icing or buttercream. Pipe borders around the cake tiers before placing other decorations on the cake so that you are not trying to work around delicate pieces.

Decorating Projects with Children

What better way to spend some quality time with your children than having them help you in the kitchen creating something beautiful and delicious. Cake decorating is an excellent opportunity for children to stretch their imaginations and gives them the opportunity to make something that they can be proud of. This chapter includes step-by-step instructions on how to make fun and creative cakes and cupcakes that are guaranteed child-pleasers. These cakes use techniques that children can do themselves, such as stamping and paint-by-number with piping gel. Be aware of a few safety precautions before starting, such as putting knives or hot cake pans out of reach. When working with children, it always helps to be well prepared. If possible, try to have all the baking equipment put away and the cake decorating supplies laid out before the children arrive and are excited to get started. This can also help with safety concerns. Make fondant plaques and cutouts beforehand and allow them to dry so they are ready to be decorated. Perhaps cut the cake into layers and put the knife away before the children come to help you decorate.

Decorating cakes and cupcakes is a fun and delicious way to spend time with your children and a great opportunity for them to use their imagination. Purchasing an assortment of candy and sprinkles for children to choose from will encourage them to be creative and make their own designs. If you have a more specific cake in mind, include your child in design decisions, such as what color to make the buttercream or which stamp to use on the sides of the cake.

When cooking or baking with younger children, it is important to make the work environment safe. Knives and pizza wheels can be very useful in baking and cake decorating, but make sure that they are in a place where only you will be able to reach them. Put hot cake pans or baking sheets into the sink and run cold water over them so that little fingers will not get burned. The same is true about hot cakes or cookies right out of the oven. Allow cakes and cookies to cool in another room or in a place that curious little hands can't reach. Talk to your child about kitchen safety before you begin and make sure that you are in the room with small children at all times.

Most baking equipment is safe for children to use, such as spatulas, palette knives (remember, these are *not* sharp), cookie cutters, and whisks. Most cake decorating tools usually are child friendly, as well. Stand mixers can be dangerous around small children if they accidentally place their hand into the bowl while the mixer is run-

OPPOSITE: Giving each child a portion of candy and the other items that will be used to decorate the cake or cupcakes keeps the activity organized and fun. Here are a few other ideas to make cake decorating fun and imaginative:

- *Use a special themed cake pan*
- *Explore candy and bulk stores for unusual candy and cake decorations*
- *Have a wide variety of food colors on hand to choose from*
- *Make a cake that focuses on a television or movie character your child loves*
- *Explore craft stores for stencils and stamps*
- *Pick a project from a modeling book and instead of using clay, use fondant to make edible figures*
- *Chill a cake in the refrigerator. The cake can then be carved into a shape or creature, such as a fish or a dragon*
- *Explore a kitchen or craft store for new cookie cutters*

ning. Hand mixers, however, give you more control and older children can use them to help mom or dad with the baking.

BELOW LEFT, DECORATING EQUIPMENT FOR WORKING WITH CHILDREN: *From top, moving clockwise: safety scissors, rolling pins, cookie cutters, popsicle sticks, tamping brushes, sponges, food color markers, gum paste tools.*

Decorating Equipment

Regardless of whether the finished product is sophisticated or fun, large or small, serious or whimsical, allow cake decorating to take your imagination and creativity to new heights. Here are some of the items needed to make and decorate beautiful cakes.

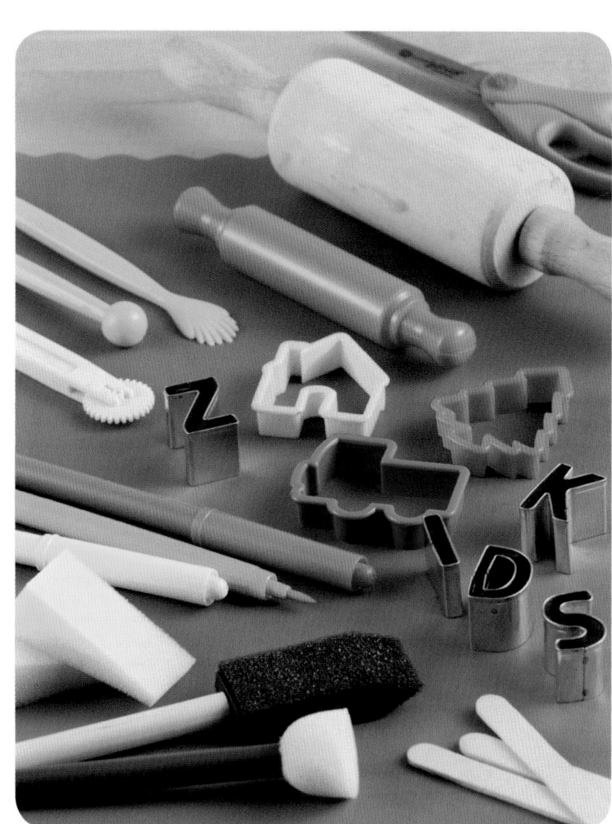

MIXERS

Numerous mixer styles are currently on the market and serve many different functions. Save your hands and use a stand mixer to make-buttercream, meringues, and royal icing. Most stand mixers come with three attachments: a whip, a paddle, and a dough hook. The whip attachment is used to make meringues, as it incorporates air and gives the egg whites volume. The paddle does not incorporate as much air as the whip, and is used to cream butter for cakes and cookies, and to add butter to meringue when making buttercream. Many hand mixers are now being sold with similar attachments to stand mixers.

KNIVES

A serrated knife is an important tool for preparing a cake to be iced and assembled. Use a serrated knife to remove any dome that might have formed during baking so that the top of the cake is a smooth, flat surface. A serrated knife can also be used to cut a cake into layers for filling. Be sure to keep the knife straight so each layer is of equal thickness. These layers can then be filled with buttercream, ganache, fruit curd, mousse, or any filling you like.

SPATULAS

Spatulas are available in a variety of different sizes and materials, such as heat-proof spatulas. For cake baking and decorating, you need a large spatula to scrape down the sides of the bowl during the mixing process and to divide the batter into the cake pans. A small, thin spatula is ideal for stirring royal icing, scraping royal icing off the sides of the bowl so that the icing doesn't dry, and transferring icing into a piping bag. You want to purchase flexible, plastic spatulas. Heat-resistant spatulas are unnecessary for cake decorating, but they do serve many other useful purposes in the kitchen.

PALETTE KNIVES/ICING SPATULAS

Palette knives are essential equipment for a cake decorator. They are available in a variety of sizes and are either flat or offset. Large and medium-sized flat spatulas are used to ice the sides of a cake and to create a smooth finish. Offset spatulas help fill the layers of a cake and ice the top surface of the cake. The size of the palette knife you use to ice a cake will depend on the size of the cake itself. You will probably feel more comfortable icing a 6- or 8-inch cake with a small palette knife, whereas a 12- or 14-inch cake might need the largest size available. Small offset palette knives are also the perfect tool for lifting delicate decorations, such as royal icing floodwork and lacework.

AT RIGHT: *Clockwise from upper left: Turntable, cardboard cake circles, drinking straws, plexiglass guides, wooden dowels, large offset palette knife, large straight palette knife, small offset palette knife, small straight palette knife, bench knife, paper doily, cake combs, rolling pin, fondant smoother, and a pizza wheel. Center, left to right: parchment cake circles, serrated knife, and rubber or silicone spatula.*

BENCH KNIFE

Bench knives have a plastic or wood handle attached to a rectangular piece of metal. Despite its name, bench knives are not sharp. They are used often in bread making to divide dough. In cake decorating, they can be used to create straight, smooth sides when finishing a cake with buttercream.

CAKE COMBS

Cake combs come in various sizes and are used to create a design in the icing on the side of the cake. Cake combs work best with buttercream icings.

PARCHMENT PAPER

Parchment paper is essential in both baking and decorating cakes. All cake pans should be lined with parchment paper to prevent sticking. Piping bags and stencils can be made out of parchment paper. Gum paste and fondant decorations should be left to dry on parchment paper dusted with cornstarch or confectioners' sugar so that they can be easily removed.

ICING/FONDANT SMOOTHER

Icing smoothers are used to smooth cakes covered with fondant or marzipan. They can be purchased at cake decorating and craft stores.

CAKE BOARDS

Cake boards are available at craft and cake decorating stores and can also be ordered online from cake decorating Web sites (see Shopping Resources, page 195). Cake boards can be purchased to fit any size or style of cake, such as squares, hearts, hexagons, and ovals. They are also available in several thicknesses, including ½, ¼, and 3/16 inch. Assemble a multi-tier cake on a ½-inch-thick cake board because the weight of the cake needs the additional support. Decorative cake boards are most readily available in only two colors: silver and gold. If these do not match the color or style of your cake design, you can cover the cake board in fondant or royal icing so that the cake board blends perfectly with the cake itself. Plastic cake plates can be purchased from craft and cake decorating stores in a variety of colors. They are usually white with a fluted edge and have four small legs that elevate the cake from the table. If white does not match your color scheme, cake plates can also be covered in fondant.

You want the cake board to be raised slightly from the table to make it easier to lift. To do this, cut a piece of ¼-inch foam core board into a circle a few inches in diameter smaller than the cake board. Glue the foam core circle to the bottom of the cake board to keep the board from moving.

AT LEFT: *Clockwise from upper left: plastic piping bags, paper cornets, a flower nail, box set of piping tips, foam pad for shaping flowers, leaf veiner, rolling pins, plastic sugar paste cutters, water pen, X-acto knife, ball tool, anger tool, knitting needle, and sewing scissors. Center, left to right: large scissors, silicone design mold, dogwood cutter, and dogwood silicone mold.*

PIPING BAGS

There are many options for a cake decorator when it comes to piping bags. You can make your own out of parchment paper or purchase disposable plastic piping bags.

Reusable plastic or nylon piping bags can also be purchased, and must be thoroughly washed after every use. If you discover a greasy film left in the piping bag after piping with buttercream, soak the bag in a bowl of hot water with a few tablespoons of white vinegar. Then rinse the bag thoroughly in hot water.

PIPING TIPS

Piping tips control the flow of the icing while forming the icing into shapes or designs. Couplers can be purchased to insert into reusable piping bags which are used to attach piping tips to the bags. The coupler allows you to change tips quickly and easily. Plain tips, which are used to pipe dots, pearl borders, or write with icings, come in sizes varying from extremely small to very large. Tips are numbered by size, so the larger the number, the larger the tip opening. Kits can be purchased at cake decorating and craft stores that have a variety of different size plain tips, as well as tips for piping roses, leaves, basket weave, stars, and many other shapes. Piping tips are available in plastic or metal and must be thoroughly cleaned to prevent any icing from drying on the inside. Small, thin brushes are available for cleaning the inside of piping tips. Make sure that metal piping tips are dried completely after being cleaned so that rust does not form on the inside of the tips. Many piping tip sets come with a rose nail, which looks like a flat metal piece attached to a screw. The nail facilitates the piping of roses and other types of flowers with icing.

AT RIGHT: *Clockwise from upper left: heart and oval cutter sets, paint brushes, tamping brush, plastic stencils, food color roller, assorted rubber and plastic stamps, plunger cutters, and assorted cutters and embossers.*

GUM PASTE TOOL SET

These sets come with several tools that are used to shape gum paste flowers. They can be purchased at craft and cake decorating stores. Similar tools are available in craft stores in the clay modeling section.

FOAM AND EGG CARTONS

Packing materials such as bubble wrap, soft foam, and egg cartons can be used to shape fondant and gum paste flowers and decorations.

STENCILS

Stencils can be made by tracing shapes onto thin plastic, cardboard, or parchment paper and then cutting out the image with either a sharp knife or scissors. Plastic stencils can also be purchased at craft stores in a huge variety of images and designs. Stencils can be used to dust images onto a cake with confectioners' sugar or cocoa powder, and they also can be placed on décor and used as a guide to paint a design with food coloring. Parchment or cardboard stencils are disposable, but plastic stencils can be cleaned and reused many times.

ABOVE: *From top and moving clockwise: paste food colors, colored sanding sugar and nonparells, jars of powdered food color, bottle of liquid food color, sponge, food color pens, color wheel, paint brushes, plastic containers for mixing food colors, and bags of colored piping gel.*

CUTTERS

A variety of metal and plastic cutters are available at cake decorating and craft stores, including petal, leaf, flower, and plunger cutters. Plunger cutters come in a variety of shapes, but tiny flowers are the most common. They are wonderful because they cut and shape the flower in one step. Cutters can be used together with plastic veiners to give petals and leaves a realistic texture. Veiners can be purchased at cake decorating stores and Internet cake decorating sites.

TAMPING BRUSH

A tamping brush is a short stick with a soft, blunt end that is available at craft stores. It is used in cake decorating to transfer a stencil design onto fondant or other décor items.

FOOD COLORS

Food colors can be found in liquid, paste, gel, and powdered form. Liquid and paste food colors are essentially interchangeable. They can be used to color royal icing or fondant, as well as to paint onto plaques or the side of a cake. To use powdered food coloring for painting, first add a small amount of liquid, such as vodka. However, powdered food color can be stirred into royal icing or kneaded into fondant without being liquefied.

LUSTER POWDERS

Luster powders are shimmery, powdered food coloring. They can be used to dust chocolate and fondant or gum paste flowers and décor items. As with other powdered food colors, adding a small amount of liquid, such as vodka, will turn the luster powder into a liquid that can be used to paint a fondant- or modeling chocolate-covered cake.

Cakes and Cupcakes

ALTHOUGH A CAKE'S decorations usually take center stage, the flavor and texture of the cake itself is just as important. This chapter includes five basic cake recipes that are easy to make: sponge, chiffon, carrot, devil's food, and hazelnut cream. Any of these recipes, or another of your choice, can be used as the base to make any of the finished cakes or cupcakes shown in this book.

A classic sponge cake is made by whipping the eggs with sugar into a thick foam and then folding in the flour and flavorings. Sponge cakes have a strong structure, making them excellent to use for multi-tiered cakes. They can be a bit dry, especially if they are over-baked or stored for long periods of time. Moisture and flavor can be added to a sponge cake by brushing each layer with a simple syrup that has had a flavoring added, such as vanilla extract or a liqueur.

Chiffon cakes are made with egg foams and have a strong structure, making them an excellent choice for tiered cakes. They are moist, flavorful, and easy to prepare.

Carrot, devil's food, and cream cakes are moist and dense. They have terrific flavor and do not need to be brushed with a flavored simple syrup. Because they have specific flavors, you might need to be more careful about the flavor of fillings you choose to pair with them. Carrot cake is moist and flavorful and is often served without filling, only with icing and décor. Devil's food cake is rich and moist and pairs well with basic flavors of chocolate and vanilla, but will do well with a thin coat of jam, such as apricot or raspberry. The hazelnut cream cake is delicately flavored and will marry well with a myriad of selections.

This chapter also explains the fundamentals of cooling, removing, and storing cakes. These techniques will ensure that you can remove your cake safely from the pan without any breakage, and that the cake stays fresh and moist until you are ready to decorate and serve it. Certain cakes, such as carrot cakes, dense butter cakes, and pound cakes, freeze very well. If you are trying to plan ahead for a party, you can bake these cakes weeks in advance and then freeze them until you are ready to decorate. Sponge cakes are naturally less moist than other cakes and should be made as close as possible to the day that the cake will be served. Sponge cakes can be frozen and then thawed, but you will need to moisten the layers with a flavored simple syrup.

OPPOSITE, CLOCKWISE FROM UPPER LEFT: *Lemon Chiffon, Vanilla Sponge, Chocolate Sponge, Devil's Food, Carrot Cake, and Hazelnut Cream Cupcakes*

Preparing Cake Pans

There are several ways to prepare a cake pan so that your cake can be easily removed. Although many cake pans advertise that they are nonstick, we recommend greasing and flouring all cake pans to be safe. Soft butter, margarine, or vegetable oil spray can be used to grease the bottoms and sides of the pans. Make sure to grease the entire pan, but do not use too much grease or it will affect the final taste of the cake and could cause it to develop a tougher crust. The same is true for flour. Although you want to ensure that the entire pan is lightly dusted, excess flour will stick to the cake and give it a powdery taste.

1. Grease the bottom and sides of the pan with soft butter, margarine, or nonstick spray. Sprinkle a handful of flour into the bottom of the pan. Shake the pan to evenly coat the bottoms and sides. Tap out any excess flour from the pan.

OR

2. Grease the sides of the pan with soft butter, margarine, or nonstick spray. Lightly dust the sides of the pan with flour. Tap out any excess flour from the pan. Using the pan as a template, cut a circle out of parchment paper (if you don't have parchment paper, you can use a brown paper bag) and place it in the bottom of the pan.

Vanilla Sponge Cake

MAKES TWO 8-INCH OR 9-INCH LAYERS, OR 24 CUPCAKES

2 cups cake flour

6 tbsp (¾ stick) unsalted butter, plus extra for greasing

1 tbsp vanilla extract

1¼ cups sugar

5 large eggs

5 large egg yolks

1. Preheat the oven to 375°F. Lightly spray two 8- or 9-inch round cake pans with a nonstick spray and line the bottoms with a round of parchment paper. For cupcakes, prepare pans with cupcake liners.

2. Sift the flour twice and set aside. Melt the butter in a saucepan over low heat. Remove from the heat, add the vanilla extract to the melted butter, and stir to combine. Set aside to cool.

3. Combine the sugar, eggs, and egg yolks in the bowl of a stand mixer and set the bowl over a pan of barely simmering water. Whisking constantly with a wire whisk, heat until the mixture is warm to the touch or reaches 120°F on a candy thermometer.

4. Remove the bowl from the heat and attach it to a stand mixer fitted with the whisk attachment. Whip the egg mixture on medium speed until the foam triples in volume and just begins to recede, about 5 minutes. Stabilize the foam on low speed for 10 minutes.

5. Fold the flour into the egg mixture using a rubber spatula. Blend a small amount of the batter into the melted butter, then fold the tempered butter back into the remaining batter.

6. Fill the prepared cake or cupcake pans about two-thirds full. Bake until the top of each layer is firm to the touch, for 8- or 9-inch cakes about 30 minutes, for cupcakes about 20 minutes.

7. Let the layers cool in the pans for a few minutes before turning out onto wire racks to finish cooling. The cakes are ready to fill and frost now, or they can be wrapped and stored at room temperature for 2 days, or frozen for up to 3 weeks.

Chocolate Sponge Cake

MAKES TWO 8-INCH OR 9-INCH LAYERS, OR 24 CUPCAKES

1½ cups cake flour

½ cup cocoa powder

6 tbsp (¾ stick) unsalted butter, plus extra for greasing

1 tbsp vanilla extract

1¼ cups sugar

5 large eggs

5 large egg yolks

1. Preheat the oven to 375°F. Lightly spray two 8- or 9-inch round cake pans with a nonstick spray and line the bottoms with a round of parchment paper. For cupcakes, prepare pans with cupcake liners.

2. Sift the flour and cocoa powder together twice and set aside. Melt the butter in a saucepan over low heat. Remove from the heat, add the vanilla extract to the melted butter, and stir to combine. Set aside to cool.

3. Combine the sugar, eggs, and egg yolks in the bowl of a stand mixer and set the bowl over a pan of barely simmering water. Whisking constantly with a wire whisk, heat until the mixture is warm to the touch or reaches 120°F on a candy thermometer.

4. Remove the bowl from the heat and attach it to a stand mixer fitted with the whisk attachment. Whip the egg mixture on medium speed until the foam triples in volume and just begins to recede, about 5 minutes. Stabilize the foam on low speed for 10 minutes.

5. Fold the flour into the egg mixture using a rubber spatula. Blend a small amount of the batter into the melted butter, then fold the tempered butter back into the remaining batter.

6. Fill the prepared cake or cupcake pans about two-thirds full. Bake until the top of each layer is firm to the touch, for 8- or 9-inch cakes about 30 minutes, for cupcakes about 20 minutes.

7. Let the layers cool in the pans for a few minutes before turning out onto wire racks to finish cooling. The cakes are ready to fill and frost now, or they can be wrapped and stored at room temperature for 2 days, or frozen for up to 3 weeks.

Lemon Chiffon Cake

MAKES TWO 8-INCH OR 9-INCH LAYERS, OR 24 CUPCAKES

3 cups cake flour

2 tsp baking powder

1 cup sugar, divided

4 large egg yolks

1 cup vegetable oil

1 cup water

½ tsp vanilla extract

Zest of 1 lemon

4 large egg whites

1. Preheat the oven to 375°F. Lightly spray two 8- or 9-inch round cake pans with a nonstick spray and line the bottoms with a round of parchment paper. For cupcakes, prepare pans with cupcake liners.

2. Sift the flour, baking powder, and half the sugar together into a large mixing bowl or stand mixer bowl and reserve.

3. In another large mixing bowl or stand mixer bowl, combine the egg yolks, oil, water, vanilla, and zest. Mix with a handheld mixer or whip attachment until thoroughly combined, about 1 minute.

4. Add the egg yolk mixture gradually to the dry ingredients, mixing with a handheld mixer or whip attachment on medium speed until a paste forms. When a paste has formed, scrape down the sides of the bowl, and continue adding the remainder of the yolk mixture until it is all incorporated. Beat for an additional 2 minutes on medium speed.

5. In a separate mixing bowl or stand mixer bowl, whip the egg whites with a clean whip attachment on medium speed until soft peaks form. Gradually add the remaining sugar while beating the egg whites and continue to beat until medium peaks form.

6. Gently blend one-third of the beaten egg whites into the egg yolk mixture to lighten it. Gently fold in the remaining egg whites.

7. Divide the batter evenly among the prepared pans.

8. Bake at 375°F until the top of a cake springs back to the touch, for 8- or 9-inch cakes about 40 minutes, for cupcakes about 20 minutes.

9. Let the layers cool in the pans for a few minutes before turning out onto wire racks to finish cooling. The cakes are ready to fill and frost now, or they can be wrapped and stored at room temperature for 2 days, or frozen for up to 3 weeks.

Chocolate Chiffon Cake

MAKES TWO 8-INCH OR 9-INCH LAYERS, OR 24 CUPCAKES

- 2½ cups cake flour
- 1 cup cocoa powder, sifted
- 2 tsp baking powder
- 1 cup sugar, divided
- 4 large egg yolks
- ¾ cup vegetable oil
- 1¼ cup water
- 1 tsp vanilla extract
- 4 large egg whites

1. Preheat the oven to 375°F. Lightly spray two 8- or 9-inch round cake pans with a nonstick spray and line the bottoms with a round of parchment paper. For cupcakes, prepare pans with cupcake liners.
2. Sift the flour, cocoa powder, baking powder, and half the sugar together into a large mixing bowl or stand mixer bowl and reserve.
3. In another large mixing bowl or stand mixer bowl, combine the egg yolks, oil, water, and vanilla. Mix with a handheld mixer or whip attachment until thoroughly combined, about 1 minute.
4. Add the egg yolk mixture gradually to the dry ingredients, mixing with a handheld mixer or whip attachment on medium speed until a paste forms. When a paste has formed, scrape down the sides of the bowl, and continue adding the remainder of the yolk mixture until it is all incorporated. Beat for an additional 2 minutes on medium speed.
5. In a separate mixing bowl or stand mixer bowl, whip the egg whites with a clean whip attachment on medium speed until soft peaks form. Gradually add the remaining sugar while beating the egg whites and continue to beat until medium peaks form.
6. Gently blend one-third of the beaten egg whites into the egg yolk mixture to lighten it. Gently fold in the remaining egg whites.
7. Divide the batter evenly among the prepared pans.
8. Bake at 375°F until the top of a cake springs back to the touch, for 8- or 9-inch cakes about 40 minutes, for cupcakes about 20 minutes.
9. Let the layers cool in the pans for a few minutes before turning out onto wire racks to finish cooling. The cakes are ready to fill and frost now, or they can be wrapped and stored at room temperature for 2 days, or frozen for up to 3 weeks.

Carrot Cake

MAKES TWO 8-INCH OR 9-INCH LAYERS, OR 24 CUPCAKES

- 2 cups cake flour
- 2 tsp baking soda
- 1 tsp iodized salt
- 1 tsp ground cinnamon
- 1¼ cups canola oil
- 1¾ cups sugar
- 4 large eggs
- 2 tsp vanilla extract
- 5 medium carrots, peeled and grated (about 3 cups grated)

1. Preheat the oven to 350°F. Lightly spray two 8- or 9-inch round cake pans with a nonstick spray and line the bottoms with a round of parchment paper. For cupcakes, prepare pans with cupcake liners.

2. Sift the flour, baking soda, salt, and cinnamon together and reserve.

3. Mix the oil, sugar, eggs, and vanilla together with a handheld beater or paddle attachment on medium speed until all ingredients are thoroughly combined, about 1 minute. Add the sifted ingredients and mix on low speed until just incorporated. Stir in the carrots by hand.

4. Divide batter evenly among the prepared pans. Bake the cakes until a skewer inserted near the center comes out clean, for 8- or 9-inch cakes 40 to 50 minutes, for cupcakes about 25 minutes.

5. Let the layers cool in the pans for a few minutes before turning out onto wire racks to finish cooling. The cakes are ready to fill and frost now, or they can be wrapped and stored at room temperature for 2 days, or frozen for up to 3 weeks.

Devil's Food Cake

MAKES TWO 8-INCH OR 9-INCH LAYERS, OR 24 CUPCAKES

- 2¾ cups sugar
- 3¼ cups cake flour
- 1½ tsp baking soda
- 1 tsp baking powder
- 5 large eggs, beaten
- 1 cup butter, melted and kept warm
- 2 cups warm water
- 1½ tsp vanilla extract
- ¼ cup cocoa powder, sifted

1. Preheat the oven to 350°F. Lightly spray two 8- or 9-inch round cake pans with a nonstick spray and line the bottoms with a round of parchment paper. For cupcakes, prepare pans with cupcake liners.

2. Sift the sugar, flour, baking soda, and baking powder together.

3. Add the beaten eggs in three additions, mixing on medium speed until each addition is fully incorporated. Scrape down the bowl as needed.

4. Add the butter and mix until evenly blended. Add the water and vanilla and mix, scraping down the bowl periodically, until a smooth batter forms. Add the cocoa powder and mix until evenly blended.

5. Divide batter evenly among the prepared pans. Bake the cakes until a skewer inserted near the center comes out clean, for 8- or 9-inch cakes 50 to 60 minutes, for cupcakes about 20 minutes.

6. Let the layers cool in the pans for a few minutes before turning out onto a wire rack to finish cooling. The cakes are ready to fill and frost now, or they can be wrapped and stored at room temperature for 2 days, or frozen for up to 3 weeks.

Devil's Food Sheet Cake

MAKES ONE 11 X 15-INCH SHEET CAKE

- 3¾ cups sugar
- 4⅓ cups cake flour
- 2 tsp baking soda
- 1 tsp baking powder
- 7 large eggs, beaten
- 1¼ cups butter, melted and kept warm
- 3 cups warm water
- 2 tsp vanilla extract
- 2 cups cocoa powder, sifted

1. Preheat the oven to 350°F. Lightly spray an 11 x 15-inch sheet pan with a nonstick spray and line the bottom with a piece of parchment paper trimmed to fit.

2. Sift the sugar, flour, baking soda, and baking powder together.

3. Add the beaten eggs in three additions, mixing on medium speed until each addition is fully incorporated. Scrape down the bowl as needed.

4. Add the butter and mix until evenly blended. Add the water and vanilla and mix, scraping down the bowl periodically, until a smooth batter forms. Add the cocoa powder and mix until evenly blended.

5. Pour the batter into the prepared pan. Bake for 50 to 60 minutes, or until a skewer inserted near the center of the cake comes out clean.

6. Let the cake cool in the pan for a few minutes before turning out onto a wire rack to finish cooling. The cake is ready to fill and frost now, or it can be wrapped and stored at room temperature for 2 days, or frozen for up to 3 weeks.

Hazelnut Cream Cake

MAKES TWO 8-INCH OR 9-INCH LAYERS, OR 24 CUPCAKES

- 1⅓ cups flour
- 1 tsp ground cinnamon
- ½ cup finely ground hazelnuts
- ½ cup buttermilk
- ½ tsp baking soda
- ¾ cup unsalted butter
- 1 cup sugar, divided
- 4 large eggs, separated
- 2 tsp vanilla extract

1. Preheat the oven to 350°F. Lightly spray two 8- or 9-inch round cake pans with a nonstick spray and line the bottoms with a round of parchment paper. For cupcakes, prepare pans with cupcake liners.

2. In a large mixing bowl, sift together the flour and cinnamon and whisk in the ground hazelnuts; set aside.

3. Combine the buttermilk and baking soda; set aside.

4. Cream the butter and ½ cup sugar together on medium speed until light in color and texture, about 3 minutes. Add the egg yolks and vanilla gradually to the creamed butter in two or three additions, scraping down the bowl as necessary and mixing until fully incorporated.

5. Add the flour-hazelnut mixture to the creamed butter and sugar in three additions, alternating with the buttermilk. Scrape the bowl down as necessary and continue to mix on medium speed until smooth and light, about 4 minutes.

6. In a clean bowl, whip the egg whites with a clean whip attachment on medium speed until soft peaks form. Gradually add the remaining sugar while beating the egg whites and continue to beat until medium peaks form.

7. Gently blend one-third of the beaten egg whites into the egg yolk mixture to lighten it. Gently fold in the remaining egg whites.

8. Divide batter evenly among the prepared pans. Bake the layers until a skewer inserted in the center comes out clean, for 8- or 9-inch cakes 30 to 45 minutes, for cupcakes about 20 minutes. Let the layers cool in the pans for a few minutes before turning out onto wire racks to finish cooling. The cakes are ready to fill and frost now, or they can be wrapped and stored at room temperature for 2 days, or frozen for up to 3 weeks.

Cooling, Removing, and Storing Cakes

COOLING CAKES

Remove the cake from the oven and place it on a cooling rack so that the air can circulate around the entire pan. Once the cake is cool to the touch, it can be removed from the pan with less chance of breakage.

REMOVING CAKES FROM THEIR PANS

1. If necessary, carefully loosen the cake from the sides of the pan with a paring knife.
2. Place one cardboard circle on top of the cake. Place one hand under the cake pan and the other hand on top of the cardboard circle. Flip the cake pan over so that the cake comes out onto the cardboard circle. Remove the parchment circle from the cake bottom if there is one. Place a second cardboard circle on the cake and flip. Remove the cardboard circle from the top of the cake.
3. If the top of the cake has a bump that needs to be cut off before icing, then place another cardboard circle on top of the inverted cake and flip it back over. Remove the first cardboard circle and cut the top of the cake so it is level (see Cutting a Cake, page 49).

STORAGE

If you are not using the cake right away, it can be wrapped in plastic wrap once it has cooled completely and stored at room temperature for up to two days, or in the freezer for up to 3 weeks.

Chapter Three

Fillings, Icings, and Meringues

THERE ARE NO limits these days with cake fillings. Just about any flavor profile, texture, and color can be accommodated. While vanilla and chocolate will always be old favorites, buttercream and ganache are excellent springboards for exciting, bold flavors, such as mango-papaya and gianduja (nut and chocolate paste). Fruit purées, flavored chocolates and pastes, candy bars, peanut butter, and extracts are just a few of the ingredients that can be used to liven up a plain buttercream or ganache.

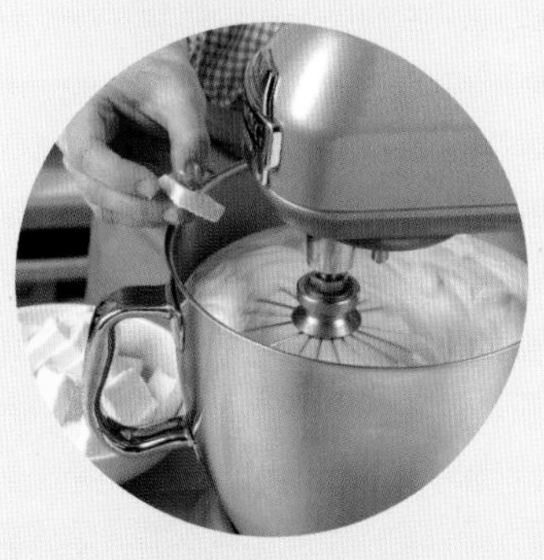

This chapter discusses several important factors to keep in mind when choosing a filling, such as flavor pairings, food safety, and the temperature where the cake will be displayed and served. Fresh fruits, such as berries and peaches, make excellent cake fillings either on their own or with an accompanying icing or whipped cream. It is best, however, to purchase these fruits when they are in season to achieve the maximum amount of flavor. Buttercream and ganache can be frozen and then reconstituted when you are ready to assemble the cake. This is a great technique for anyone who likes to be prepared ahead of time. It can also come in handy to have a container of buttercream in the freezer in the event of a surprise bake sale or a birthday party.

Choosing a Cake Filling

Two important criteria to consider when choosing a cake filling are the length of time the cake will be out of the refrigerator before serving and how the filling will pair with the flavor of the cake.

FOOD SAFETY

A cake that is to be on display for more than two hours, especially if it is going to be outside, should not have a pastry cream, curd, or whipped cream filling. These fillings are not shelf stable and also can cause the cake to lose its shape if the fillings become too warm. The ideal fillings for a wedding or special occasion cake that is to be on display are Italian and Swiss meringue buttercreams because both are stable and can sit at room temperature for several hours. Use pasteurized egg whites when making the buttercream if the cake will be on display for more than four hours.

FLAVOR PAIRINGS

Pairing different cake and filling flavors is yet another way to stretch your creativity and is based entirely on your own preferences. Explore new pairings with flavor combinations you might not have tried before. The following are a few guidelines and suggestions to help you get started:

More acidic fruit flavors, such as passion fruit and lemon, tend to pair best with a mild cake flavor, such as vanilla. Deep, strong flavors, such as mocha and caramel, hold their own beautifully when paired with rich, chocolate cake. While carrot cake is traditionally filled with cream cheese frosting, try adding additional flavors to the frosting, such as orange zest or grated, fresh ginger. Chocolate ganache is an elegant filling on its own, but the flavor can be dramatically changed by the addition of extracts, brewed espresso, or fruit purées. Cheesecake batter of any flavor can be baked into layers approximately 1 inch thick and used as a substitute for a buttercream filling. Simply alternate layers of cake and cheesecake for a unique and delicious flavor and texture combination. Try alternating different flavors of fillings throughout a cake in order to create an attractive cross section once the cake is sliced. For example, using three types of curds, such as lemon, raspberry, and blueberry, to fill a light vanilla or citrus cake will create a very impressive flavor and color combination. An additional factor to consider when choosing a cake filling is the density of the cake itself. A heavy pound cake may not pair as well with an airy mousse as would a light sponge or chiffon cake.

OPPOSITE: *Back row, left to right: Vanilla Pastry Cream, Chocolate Pastry Cream, Lemon Curd; middle row, left to right: Coffee Buttercream, Vanilla Buttercream, Pistachio Buttercream; clockwise at front, starting at lower left: fresh mixed berries, strawberries, Soft Ganache, apricot jam, raspberry jam.*

USING FRESH FRUIT IN FILLINGS

Fresh, ripe fruit is the perfect expression of summer. Fresh berries are an excellent accompaniment to a citrus curd and work best with whipped cream and buttercream fillings because they do not contain as much water as other fruits, such as peaches. To successfully use sliced, moist fruit like peaches, allow both sides of the slices to dry on pieces of paper towel so that they are not too wet. The water in fruit and the fat in buttercream and whipped cream do not mix well. If the fruit is too wet, the cake layers might slide off of each other. Use fruit that is ripe and in season for the maximum flavor. Avoid frozen fruit because they contain excess water and are more likely to damage the other fillings in your cake. If frozen fruit is all that is available, prepare a cooked fruit filling, such as one you might use for a pie, so that the excess water does not leach out of the fruit onto the other fillings. A classic example is whipped cream paired with a cooked cherry filling in a black forest cake.

SWEETENED WHIPPED CREAM

Whipped cream is quite bland on its own, but easily can be improved with the addition of sugar (granulated or confectioners') and a flavoring, such as vanilla, espresso, and chocolate. To give the cream a sophisticated appearance, flavor it with vanilla paste that will dot the white cream with flecks of black vanilla seeds. Vanilla paste can be purchased at gourmet food stores. Use sweetened whipped cream to pipe onto a cake so that the decorations taste as delicious as the cake itself.

Vanilla Pastry Cream

MAKES 1 POUND OR ABOUT 3 CUPS

⅓ cup cornstarch

1 cup sugar

3 cups whole milk

6 large egg yolks, lightly beaten

¼ tsp salt

1 tbsp vanilla extract

3 tbsp butter

VARIATIONS:

• ***CHOCOLATE:*** Add 4 ounces melted bittersweet chocolate to the warm finished cream.

1. Combine the cornstarch with ¼ cup of the sugar. Mix in ½ cup of the milk. Blend the egg yolks into the mixture, stirring until completely smooth.

2. Combine the remaining milk with the remaining sugar and the salt in a saucepan over medium heat and bring to a boil. Remove the pan from the heat.

3. Temper the egg mixture by gradually adding about one-third of the hot milk while whisking constantly. Add the tempered egg mixture to the remaining milk in the pan. Cook over medium heat while stirring constantly until the whisk leaves a trail in the cream and the mixture returns to a boil, about 7 minutes.

5. Remove the pan from the heat, stir in the vanilla and the butter, and pour the mixture into a shallow container to cool. Place a piece of plastic wrap directly on the surface of the pastry cream to prevent a skin from forming.

6. Cover and store in the refrigerator for up to 3 days.

Lemon Curd

MAKES 1 POUND OR ABOUT 3 CUPS

1 cup butter, cubed
1 cup sugar
1 cup lemon juice
Zest of 3 lemons
10 large egg yolks

1. Combine half of the butter, half of the sugar, the lemon juice, and zest and bring to a boil over medium heat, stirring gently to dissolve the sugar.
2. Meanwhile, blend the egg yolks with the remaining sugar. Temper by gradually adding about one-third of the lemon juice mixture, stirring constantly with a whip. Return the tempered egg mixture to the saucepan. Continue cooking, stirring constantly, until the whisk leaves a trail in the curd. Remove from the heat.
3. Stir in the remaining butter.
4. Strain the curd into a shallow container or bowl. Cover with plastic wrap placed directly on the surface of the curd. Cool over an ice bath.
5. Store the curd, covered, in the refrigerator for up to 3 days.

VARIATIONS:

- ***ORANGE, LIME, OR GRAPEFRUIT CURD:*** Replace the lemon juice and zest with the juice and zest of the citrus fruit you wish to use. If making Orange Curd, reduce the sugar by 2 tablespoons.
- ***RASPBERRY CURD:*** Replace the lemon juice with unsweetened raspberry purée and omit the zest.
- ***BLUEBERRY CURD:*** Replace the lemon juice with unsweetened blueberry purée and omit the zest.

Ganache

Ganache is an emulsion of chocolate and heavy cream that can serve many purposes depending on the consistency of the ganache. Soft and hard ganache can be achieved by varying the ratio of chocolate to cream.

Hard ganache is the most versatile and can be used for glazing, filling, and decorating a cake. Soft ganache, which is similar in consistency to mousse, can be used as a cake filling if it is whipped to a spreadable consistency.

Once hard ganache has come together, allow the mixture to thicken either in a cool place or the refrigerator. To make the ganache easier to work with, it can be paddled lightly with a hand or stand mixer until it is light and more spreadable. Hard ganache can be placed in a piping bag and piped into designs, leaves, and small flowers in a similar manner to buttercream. Ganache does not pipe easily into larger roses, but modeling chocolate roses pair nicely with a cake that has ganache décor.

Ganache is not readily available in stores, but it is simple to prepare. By making it yourself you can control the quality of the chocolate used as well as the consistency of the ganache. Ganache can be refrigerated in airtight containers for up to 3 weeks and in the freezer for up to 2 months.

Hard Ganache

MAKES 5 POUNDS OR ABOUT 8 CUPS

4 lb dark chocolate, finely chopped

4 cups heavy cream

1. Place the chocolate in a stainless-steel bowl.
2. Bring the heavy cream just to a simmer. Pour the hot cream over the chocolate, allow to stand for 1 minute, and stir until the chocolate is thoroughly melted.
3. The ganache can be used immediately, or it can be covered and stored under refrigeration, then warmed prior to use.

Soft Ganache

MAKES 3 POUNDS 6 OUNCES OR ABOUT 6 CUPS

20 oz dark chocolate, finely chopped

4 cups heavy cream

VARIATIONS:
Substitute milk chocolate or white chocolate for the dark chocolate.

1. Place the chocolate in a stainless-steel bowl.
2. Bring the heavy cream to a simmer. Pour the hot cream over the chocolate. Allow to stand for 1 minute, and then gently stir to blend. Allow to cool completely.
3. Cover with plastic wrap and refrigerate overnight before using.
4. Whip the ganache to desired peaks for use.

NOTE: For a lighter flavored ganache, add an equal amount of cream (by volume) to the chilled ganache before whipping.

Italian and Swiss Meringue Buttercream

Buttercream essentially is a meringue with soft butter and a flavoring added to it. Italian and Swiss meringue buttercreams are much lighter in texture and mouth feel than American buttercream, which is simply soft butter beaten with confectioners' sugar. Italian meringue buttercream involves cooking a sugar syrup to the soft ball stage (240°F), and then streaming the hot sugar into a soft peak meringue. Swiss meringue buttercream is easier and faster to make; the sugar and egg whites are combined at the beginning and heated until the sugar dissolves (140°F) before the meringue is whipped to glossy, medium peaks and the butter is added.

Both types of buttercream are very stable and are ideal for multi-tiered cakes, especially if they are going to be on display for several hours. Buttercream should have a very fluffy consistency, so do not be afraid to whip it on high speed. Also, buttercream is best served at room temperature and not cold.

The exterior of a cake can be decorated with small buttercream dots or a more intricate design. Vines, flowers, and leaves can be piped directly onto a cake. Buttercream roses can be piped separately on a flower nail, allowed to set, and then transferred onto a cake for a professional finish.

Italian and Swiss meringue buttercreams are easily flavored with extracts, chocolate, coffee, or fruit purées. They can be colored with regular food colors, but oil-based food colors will provide a stronger and brighter color. The versatility of these buttercreams make them an excellent choice for filling, icing, and decorating a wide variety of cakes.

Although many varieties of icings can be purchased, Italian and Swiss meringue buttercreams are unavailable in stores and must be handmade. The results, however, are well worth the effort. Buttercream can be refrigerated for approximately 1 week and frozen for several weeks in an airtight container.

ABOVE: *Meringues, from top to bottom: stiff peak, medium peak, and soft peak*

Swiss Meringue Buttercream

MAKES ABOUT 6 CUPS

4 large egg whites
1 cup sugar
2 cups unsalted butter, cubed, at room temperature
2 tsp vanilla extract

1. Put the egg whites and sugar in the clean, grease-free bowl of a stand mixer fitted with the whisk attachment and stir together until the sugar is blended into the egg whites.

2. Place the bowl over a saucepan of simmering water and stir frequently until the sugar dissolves and the mixture reaches 140 to 150°F.

3 Transfer the bowl to the mixer and beat on high speed until the meringue and the bowl are cool to the touch.

4. Add the cubed butter gradually, mixing after each addition until fully incorporated and scraping down the sides of the bowl as necessary. Blend in the vanilla. The buttercream is ready for use or may be tightly covered and stored in the refrigerator for up to 1 week.

VARIATIONS:

- ***CHOCOLATE BUTTERCREAM:*** Add 4 ounces bittersweet chocolate, melted and slightly cooled, to 2½ cups prepared buttercream.
- ***WHITE CHOCOLATE BUTTERCREAM:*** Add 2 ounces white chocolate, melted and slightly cooled, to 2½ cups prepared buttercream.
- ***COFFEE BUTTERCREAM:*** Add 2 tablespoons instant coffee reconstituted in 2 tablespoons of warm water to 2½ cups prepared buttercream.
- ***PISTACHIO BUTTERCREAM:*** Add 2 ounces pistachio paste to 2½ cups prepared buttercream.

Repairing Separated Buttercream

Separated buttercream will appear lumpy and greasy. Buttercream usually separates because it was too cold when it was mixed. This can be easily fixed by warming up the bottom of the metal mixing bowl over a low flame or with hot water and whipping the buttercream at the same time. This will warm up the buttercream and will bring it back together.

Italian Buttercream

MAKES ABOUT 7 CUPS

2 cups sugar

½ cup water

8 large egg whites

4 cups unsalted butter, cubed, room temperature

1 tbsp vanilla extract

1. Combine 1½ cups of the sugar with the water in a heavy-bottomed saucepan and bring to a boil over medium-high heat, stirring to dissolve the sugar. Continue cooking without stirring to the soft ball stage (240°F).

2. Meanwhile, place the egg whites in the bowl of an electric mixer fitted with the wire whip attachment.

3. When the sugar syrup has reached approximately 230°F, whip the egg whites on medium speed to soft peak consistency. Gradually add the remaining ½ cup of sugar and beat until the egg whites hold to medium peaks.

4. When the sugar syrup reaches 240°F, immediately pour it into a heatproof glass measuring cup with a pouring spout. This will allow better control of the flow of the hot syrup into the egg whites. You can also stream the hot syrup into the egg whites directly from the pot, if desired. Pour the sugar syrup into the egg whites with the mixer running on medium speed. As soon as all of the syrup has been added, increase the speed to high and continue to whip until the meringue has cooled to room temperature.

5. Add the cubed butter gradually, mixing after each addition until fully incorporated and scraping down the sides of the bowl as necessary. Blend in the vanilla. The buttercream is ready for use or may be tightly covered and stored in the refrigerator for up to 1 week.

BELOW LEFT: *Stream the cooked sugar into the soft peak egg whites on medium-high speed.* **CENTER:** *Add the butter, a piece at a time, while beating constantly.* **RIGHT:** *Top to bottom, buttercream that is cold and lumpy, buttercream that is of the desired smooth consistency, and buttercream that is too warm and runny.*

Swiss Meringue

MAKES ABOUT 6 CUPS

4 large egg whites
1 cup sugar

1. Put the egg whites and sugar in the clean, grease-free bowl of a stand mixer fitted with a whisk attachment and stir together until the sugar is blended into the whites.

2. Place the bowl over a saucepan of simmering water and stir frequently until the mixture reaches 140°F.

3. Transfer the bowl to the mixer and beat on high speed until the meringue is thick and glossy and has the desired peak (soft, medium, or stiff) according to its intended use.

Italian Meringue

MAKES ABOUT 7 CUPS

¾ cup sugar
¼ cup water
5 large egg whites

1. Combine ½ cup of the sugar with the water in a heavy saucepan. Cook over medium-high heat without stirring until the mixture reaches 230°F. At that time, place the egg whites in the bowl of a stand mixer fitted with a whisk attachment and whip on medium speed to soft peak consistency.

2. Add the remaining ¼ cup of sugar and beat the meringue to medium peaks. When the sugar mixture reaches the soft ball stage, 240°F, pour it into the measuring cup, then into the meringue in a slow, steady stream on low speed. Increase the speed to high and whip until the meringue cools to room temperature and has the desired peak.

Reconstituting Cold Buttercream

Cold buttercream must be reconstituted before it is whipped, as whipping cold buttercream will cause the fat and the water in the icing to separate. Use the following method to quickly reconstitute cold buttercream:

1. Cut the block of buttercream into chunks.

2. Warm the buttercream in the microwave in short intervals. Start at 5 second intervals and watch carefully, the duration of time in the microwave will vary from oven to oven. Stir the buttercream gently with a spatula between intervals.

3. As the buttercream begins to soften, transfer the soft buttercream to the bowl of an electric mixer. The buttercream around the sides and at the bottom of the container will soften first.

4. Beat the soft buttercream on medium speed until smooth. The buttercream can then be flavored or colored as needed.

Chapter Four

Icing and Décor Mediums

A CAKE DECORATOR has many choices when it comes to both the outside and the inside of a cake. A particular décor item, such as a heart shaped box or a rose, can be made out of several different types of décor mediums including fondant, gum paste, marzipan, and pastillage. Regardless of whether you are stamping, embossing, painting, or modeling, there are a variety of décor mediums to choose from that will best suit your project.

This chapter describes various décor mediums and their properties, and also gives details about usage, storage, and where they can be purchased. Several factors should be kept in mind when choosing a décor medium for a project. These include the medium's durability, flavor, texture, and ability to hold up under certain temperature conditions. For example, if you are planning to serve a cake on a very hot summer day, you may choose to make flowers out of gum paste or modeling chocolate rather than buttercream.

In addition to icings and sugar pastes, fruits and flowers, berries, and garnishes made of tempered or coating chocolate make impressive cake décor. A combination of several mediums is also very effective if they complement each other. By learning as much as possible about the different décor mediums and experimenting with them, you can take your cake decorating creativity to new heights.

Modeling Chocolate

BELOW: *Décor mediums, from top to bottom: gum paste, white modeling chocolate, dark modeling chocolate, fondant, and pastillage.*

Modeling chocolate is an excellent medium for shaping roses, leaves, ribbons, bows, and three-dimensional figures. Modeling chocolate can also be rolled out to enrobe a cake in a manner similar to fondant. Because modeling chocolate dries quickly, it is best to work with small pieces at a time. Take a section of the modeling chocolate and knead it until it is pliable. If the modeling chocolate becomes too hard to work with, it can be warmed in the microwave in 10-second intervals until it is malleable again. Be careful not to overheat the modeling chocolate, because this will damage its consistency. Modeling chocolate garnishes are well suited for a chocolate cake or one with a chocolate filling because the décor indicates what flavors will be found inside the cake. Modeling chocolate is an extremely versatile décor medium, because it blends well with chocolate glazed cakes as well as buttercream- and fondant-covered cakes. Modeling chocolate and marzipan decorations also pair nicely together. Modeling chocolate is unavailable in stores, but it is simple to prepare and by making it yourself you can control the type and quality of the chocolate used. Paste and liquid food colors can be used to color modeling chocolate. To store modeling chocolate, shape it into a log and thoroughly wrap in plastic. It can be kept in the refrigerator for up to 1 month.

Dark Modeling Chocolate

MAKES 1½ POUNDS

1 cup corn syrup, warm

1 lb dark chocolate, melted and still warm

1. Add the warm corn syrup to the warm chocolate and use a spatula to blend into a smooth paste.

2. Pour the chocolate mixture on a tray to cool. Cover with plastic wrap and refrigerate for at least 1 hour.

3. Shape into a log and wrap well in plastic wrap. Store the modeling chocolate in the refrigerator for up to 1 month.

4. To use the modeling chocolate, knead it until smooth and pliable, using a light dusting of sifted cocoa powder, if necessary, to prevent sticking. Be careful not to overwork the chocolate or it will become oily.

White Modeling Chocolate

MAKES 2 POUNDS

1 cup corn syrup, warm

1½ lb white chocolate, melted and still warm

1. Add the warm corn syrup to the warm chocolate and use a spatula to blend into a smooth paste. For white modeling chocolate it is very important to avoid overmixing.

2. Pour the chocolate mixture on a tray to cool, cover with plastic wrap, then refrigerate for at least 1 hour.

3. Shape into a log and wrap well in plastic wrap. Store the modeling chocolate in the refrigerator for up to 1 month.

4. To use the modeling chocolate, knead it until smooth and pliable, using a light dusting of sifted confectioners' sugar, if necessary, to prevent sticking. Be careful not to overwork the chocolate or it will become oily.

BELOW LEFT: Stream the warm corn syrup into the melted chocolate. CENTER: Stir the corn syrup into the melted chocolate; the chocolate will appear slightly greasy, but the mixture will come together as you continue to stir. RIGHT: The modeling chocolate will come together in a ball once the chocolate and the corn syrup have been completely blended.

WORKING WITH DÉCOR MEDIUMS

Fondant, gum paste, pastillage, and marzipan are excellent décor mediums. Fondant and marzipan can also be rolled into sheets and used to cover a cake to achieve a smooth, polished finish. When rolling out sugar pastes for covering or for decorating, confectioners' sugar or cornstarch is needed to prevent the paste from sticking to the work surface. A sieve can be used to dust the work surface, or fill a piece of cheesecloth with confectioners' sugar or cornstarch and tie it securely to form a dusting pouch. If you do not have cheesecloth, a brand new pair of panty hose or stockings can be cut just above the ankle, filled with sugar or cornstarch, and knotted at the top to close. Pat the dusting pouch over the work surface to achieve a thin layer of sugar or cornstarch that is free of lumps. While working with gum paste it may become dry and cracked. To return the paste to its original consistency, knead a small amount of vegetable shortening or water into the gum paste until it is smooth.

Gum Paste

Gum paste's elastic consistency allows the material to be stretched and shaped. Gum paste decorations dry extremely hard; but the thinner the garnish, the more delicate it becomes. Its strength and elasticity make gum paste an ideal medium for making roses, wired flowers, plaques, ribbons, bows, and models, such as a bride and groom cake topper. Gum paste can be easily colored with paste or powdered food coloring, and dusting gum paste decorations with powdered coloring creates an impressive shading effect. Gum paste decorations are best suited for cakes covered in fondant, marzipan, or modeling chocolate because of their polished finish. Gum paste makes extremely elegant décor, but keep in mind that it is not very palatable, and will not likely be eaten. Gum paste mixes and ready-made gum pastes are available at cake decorating and craft stores. To store gum paste, roll it into a log and coat with a thin layer of vegetable shortening. Wrap the gum paste twice in plastic wrap and store in the refrigerator for several months. Gum paste decorations should be left to dry on parchment paper dusted with cornstarch or confectioners' sugar so that they do not stick to the surface. If you have extra decorations that you want to store, place them in a cardboard box, such as a shoe box, and store them in a dry place. Storing gum paste in plastic containers will make the decorations soft.

Marzipan

Marzipan is both a flavorful and a versatile décor medium. Be aware that marzipan contains almonds and, therefore, is unsuitable for certain individuals with nut allergies. Marzipan can be rolled out and used to enrobe a cake and is the traditional covering for fruit cake. Marzipan is soft and malleable to work with but dries very quickly. It is ideal for shaping roses, leaves, bows, and other figures. Miniature marzipan fruits are a classic decoration for cakes and simple to make. Figures tend to require a firmer marzipan to hold their shape, which can be achieved by kneading some confectioners' sugar into the marzipan.

Marzipan can be colored with paste food colors and then dusted with powdered food colors to create shading. Be careful not to overwork marzipan while rolling or shaping it, because the marzipan may become oily and will lose its smooth appearance and texture. If this happens, knead a small amount of simple syrup or clear corn syrup into the marzipan, which will bind the marzipan back together. If necessary, more confectioners' sugar can be kneaded into the marzipan to restore its original consistency. Decorations made of marzipan are suitable for chocolate glazed cakes, buttercream- and fondant-covered cakes, as well as pound cakes and fruitcakes that may or may not be covered. If the marzipan décor will be eaten, ensure that the almond flavor will pair well with the flavor of the cake. For example, marzipan may not suit a lemon chiffon cake, but it will match nicely with a chocolate, vanilla, or nut-flavored cake.

Marzipan is widely available ready-made. Wrap marzipan thoroughly in plastic wrap and store in the refrigerator for up to 6 months. Molded and dried marzipan can be stored in an airtight container in a cool place for up to 6 months. If you detect an unpleasant odor in the marzipan, simply discard it. This odor occurs if the almond oil becomes rancid.

Pastillage

Pastillage is a sugar paste stabilized with gelatin and cornstarch. It can be rolled into a sheet and cut into various shapes and designs. Pastillage dries extremely hard and is therefore an excellent medium for making sugar boxes and other three-dimensional decorations. Because pastillage can absorb moisture from buttercream cakes, pastillage decorations are best suited for fondant or modeling chocolate covered cakes.

Pastillage shapes or designs can be dried, painted with food coloring, or decorated with royal icing, and then adhered with royal icing to the top or sides of a cake.

Pastillage firms quickly and the best results are achieved by using the product the day it is made. Pastillage is best made at home because of how quickly the product dries. Pastillage can be wrapped in plastic wrap as directed below and stored in the refrigerator, for up to 1 month.

Pastillage

MAKES 1 POUND 2 OUNCES

2 tbsp water, cold
1 tsp gelatin, powdered
6 oz confectioners' sugar, plus additional as needed
1½ tbsp cornstarch

1. Bloom gelatin in water 5 to 10 minutes in the bowl of a stand mixer. Melt over a hot water bath until the gelatin has dissolved and is hot.

2. Sift together the sugar and cornstarch. Add two-thirds of the dry ingredients to the gelatin mixture and mix until the dry ingredients have been moistened. Continue to add the dry ingredients a little bit at a time until a dough is formed. It should be soft but not wet. Adjust consistency with additional sifted powdered sugar as needed.

4. Roll out the pastillage to form decorations or store in the refrigerator for later use. To store, form the pastillage into a log, wrap tightly with plastic wrap, then a damp paper towel, and then with plastic wrap again.

DÉCOR MEDIUMS TO PURCHASE

For ease and convenience, there are a variety of icings and décor mediums that can be purchased on the web and in craft and cake decorating stores. Because traditional royal icing uses egg whites, you can purchase high-quality royal icing mixes that often require only the addition of water and are safe at room temperature. Ready-prepared fondant comes flavored with vanilla or chocolate and can also be purchased in other colors, such as ivory. For small projects 24-ounce packages are available and larger boxes starting at 5 pounds can be purchased for multi-tiered cakes. Excellent-quality marzipan can be purchased, usually in tubes, from most grocery stores. For decorating in a pinch, a variety of ready prepared icings are available in numerous flavors. For piping decorations, choose a firm icing that will hold its shape. For more information about purchasing ready-made décor mediums, refer to Shopping Resources, page 195.

Fondant

Fondant is used principally to enrobe cakes because it creates a smooth, porcelain-like finish. It can be used to cover multi-tiered wedding cakes or small, 6-inch birthday cakes. Before working with a piece of fondant, remove any crust that may have formed around the exterior so it does not get kneaded into the fondant and ruin its smooth consistency. Fondant can be shaped into molded flowers, but is unsuitable for wired flowers because it is not as strong as gum paste. Fondant can also be used to make plaques, ribbons, bows, and other figures. You can also make fondant boxes if pastillage is unavailable. Fondant can be purchased at cake decorating, craft, and online stores. Fondant is also available in different size packages to accommodate large and small projects. Fondant can be easily colored with liquid, paste, and powdered food coloring to fit any color scheme and can also be purchased in white, ivory, and chocolate brown. Fondant can be stored at room temperature, thoroughly covered in plastic wrap, for several months. Fondant decorations should be left to dry on parchment paper dusted with cornstarch or confectioners' sugar so that they do not stick to the surface. If you have extra decorations that you want to store, place them in a cardboard box, such as a shoe box, and store them in a dry place. Storing fondant in plastic containers will make the decorations soft.

Piping Gel

Piping gel is a versatile décor medium that can be used to pipe messages as well as outline or fill designs on cakes, cupcakes, and cookies. It can easily be colored with liquid or paste food coloring. Piping gel designs can be piped onto sheets of acetate and left to dry overnight, peeled off when dry, and placed on iced cakes, cupcakes, or cookies.

Piping gel can be purchased in small tubs at cake decorating, craft, and cooking stores. Like other foods, piping gel is perishable and should be stored in a dry place.

Chocolate Piping Gel

3 oz melted dark chocolate

1 lb piping gel

1. Stir the melted chocolate into the piping gel.
2. Strain the mixture through cheesecloth by placing a piece of cloth in a small bowl; spoon the chocolate piping gel on top, close the cheesecloth around the gel, twist it closed, and squeeze the cloth until all the gel has been forced through.
3. Store in a closed container for up to 5 days.

Royal Icing

Royal icing's strength and the fact that it dries extremely hard makes it ideal for making piped décor, as well as for attaching other decorations to a cake. Royal icing can be used to pipe borders around a cake, to make floodwork, to pipe leaves, flowers, and vines onto a cake, and to make intricate string work. Different styles of piping tips are available to achieve hundreds of shapes and designs with royal icing or buttercream. Royal icing décor and piping are best suited for a cake covered in fondant, marzipan, or modeling chocolate. Royal icing can be made with fresh egg whites or pasteurized egg whites to eliminate any concerns about safety. Excellent royal icing mixes are available in stores if you do not have time to prepare a batch at home.

Royal icing can be colored with gel, liquid, or powdered food coloring. It is usually not flavored because it is more of a décor medium than a frosting.

To store royal icing, place a dampened paper towel directly on top of the icing and then cover the bowl with a layer of plastic wrap.

Royal Icing

MAKES ABOUT 1 CUP

2 large egg whites

⅛ tsp cream of tartar

2½ cups confectioners' sugar, sifted

Liquid or paste food coloring(s) as needed (optional)

NOTE: You may prefer to use pasteurized egg whites in this recipe to eliminate any food safety concerns.

1. In the clean, grease-free bowl of a stand mixer fitted with the whisk attachment, beat the egg whites on low speed just until they become loose, about 1 minute. Add the cream of tartar and continue mixing on low speed until the egg whites become frothy, about 2 minutes. Add the confectioners' sugar gradually with the mixer on low speed. Continue to mix until the icing holds a soft peak and is dull in appearance, about 2 minutes. The icing is ready to use for piping lines. Or, add a small amount of water until the icing reaches looser consistency for flooding, or filling in, an outline. If desired, divide the icing among smaller bowls and add food coloring(s).

2. If you won't be using the icing right away, take the following steps to keep the icing from drying out: Clean the sides of the bowl or container to remove any drips; if a dry crust develops on the bowl, small pieces can drop into the icing and clog the tip of your pastry bag or parchment paper cone. Place a dampened paper towel directly on the surface of the icing and then cover the bowl very tightly with plastic wrap. Refrigerate for up to 5 days.

Fresh Flowers and Fruit for Décor

FLOWER DÉCOR

The most important factor in choosing fresh flowers for cakes is that they are safe to come into contact with food, meaning they are free of natural toxins and pesticides.

Here is a partial list of edible flowers that will add a dramatic touch to any cake:

- Pansies
- Roses
- Mint and other herbs
- Lavender
- Violets
- Daylilies
- Marigolds

If purchasing flowers from a florist, be sure to ask which flowers are food safe before selecting the ones you will put on your cake. Although they are beautiful, avoid calla lilies, daffodils, sweet peas, and orchids, because they contain natural toxins. Many edible flowers, such as pansies and rose petals, can now be found prewashed in packages at gourmet food stores. If you have edible flowers in your garden and you do not use pesticides, feel free to look for cake decorations in your own backyard.

FRUIT DÉCOR

Fruit should be well washed and thoroughly dried before used to decorate a cake. Small fruits, such as cherries, apricots, and berries, are ideal because they put so little weight onto the cake and will not disrupt the icing. Larger fruit is best placed on fondant-covered cakes because the weight is less likely to make an indent in the fondant, as it would in buttercream. Using fruit as a décor item has the added benefit of allowing the decorator to indicate what ingredients and flavors are inside the cake itself. Avoid confusing your guests by decorating with fruit that does not match or pair with the flavors in your cake, such as decorating a black forest cake with orange segments. Sliced, fresh fruit should be used as garnishes only when they are ripe and most flavorful. Once the flesh of the fruit is exposed to the air, a process known as oxidation will cause it to discolor and turn brown. This can be avoided by simply brushing the sliced fruit with a thin layer of melted apricot or apple jelly, which prevents the air from coming into contact with the fruit. The jelly also gives the fruit a glossy, polished finish and adds another flavor dimension to the cake. Orange and grapefruit segments have the advantage of not oxidizing, but a thin layer of jelly, such as citrus marmalade, should be applied to these fruits to keep the segments moist and shiny.

Sugaring Flowers and Fruit

Sugared flowers, petals, fruit, and citrus peel are sophisticated additions to a cake or dessert plate and are simple to make. Sugared mint is decadent and its vibrant green color complements many flowers. If you are concerned about using uncooked egg white, reconstitute 2 teaspoons of albumen powder (powdered egg white) with 2 tablespoons of warm water. Albumen substitute dissolves faster than pure albumen and is lighter in color. Lightly beat the reconstituted egg white as you would a fresh egg white and proceed with the sugaring as directed.

1. Fill a bowl with a beaten egg white and another bowl with super fine (also called castor) sugar.
2. Cut the stems of the flowers to the desired length and ensure that the fruit and the flower petals are completely dry.
3. Using a pastry brush, coat the entire piece of fruit or flower with a light coating of egg white. A paint brush can be used for delicate pieces, such as petals, as long as the brush is brand new or has only been used with food.
4. Using a spoon or your fingers, sprinkle sugar over the entire fruit or flower. Shake lightly to remove any excess sugar and dry on pieces of paper towel for 3 to 4 hours.

Tempering Chocolate

The process of tempering chocolate changes the crystal structure of the cocoa butter, thereby making it stronger and shinier, and also prevents it from blooming. Have you ever seen a piece of chocolate speckled with white dots? Known as fat bloom, these white dots occur when the cocoa butter separates from the other ingredients and crystallizes on the surface, forming white dots or a grayish film. The chocolate is not spoiled, so simply melting the chocolate will incorporate the cocoa butter back into the other ingredients. However, fat bloom damages the chocolate's appearance and makes the chocolate garnish unusable for decoration. Store-bought chocolate is already tempered, which is why it has its shiny, bloom-free appearance. Once melted, however, the chocolate is no longer in temper and must be brought back into the tempered state to make decorations. There are several different techniques for tempering chocolate, including seeding and the block method, which involve heating, cooling, and stirring the melted chocolate to form stable cocoa butter crystals.

SEEDING

Seeding is a simple method for tempering chocolate. Be sure to use all of the same brand and type of chocolate for each batch to ensure the best results.

1. Chop the chocolate finely into pieces. Place two-thirds of the chocolate in a bowl or the top of a double boiler and melt over gently simmering water, reserving the rest of the chocolate to use as seed.
2. Remove the bowl from the heat. Stir the chocolate and allow it to cool slightly.
3. Add a small handful of the reserved chocolate pieces to the bowl of melted chocolate, stirring until completely melted and incorporated.

4. Add another, smaller handful of chocolate pieces and stir until they are melted. Repeat this process, adding fewer and fewer pieces of tempered chocolate with each addition until the melted chocolate is body temperature (when the chocolate touches your skin it should feel neither warm nor cool). You do not want chunks in the tempered chocolate, so as it cools make sure to add only a few pieces of tempered chocolate at a time so they fully melt.

5. To check if the chocolate is in temper, dip a knife or small offset spatula into the chocolate and allow it to set. If it is fully tempered, the chocolate on the knife will set in 3 minutes or less and will have a shiny, streak-free appearance. If the chocolate does not set or is very streaky, continue stirring in small pieces of chocolate. If necessary, warm the chocolate slightly over the simmering water so that you can add larger additions of tempered chocolate pieces.

6. To hold the chocolate in temper, stir it often, keeping the chocolate in the center of the bowl and off of the sides. As the chocolate thickens, you will need to warm the chocolate by placing it over the simmering water in 3-second intervals. Be careful not to heat the chocolate out of temper.

VARIATION:

BLOCK METHOD: Chop two-thirds of the chocolate, leaving the remaining third in a large block. Melt the chopped chocolate over a double boiler. Add the reserved block of chocolate and stir constantly until the chocolate reaches body temperature. Proceed with steps 5 and 6 of the method at left.

If you do not have the time to temper chocolate, you can purchase a product called coating chocolate, which contains other vegetable fats for easier handling. Coating chocolate can be melted and piped and will set without tempering. Colored confectionery coatings can also be purchased and will set up on their own when melted and piped. These chocolates are available at cake decorating stores, as well as online stores.

Chapter Five

Cake Assembly

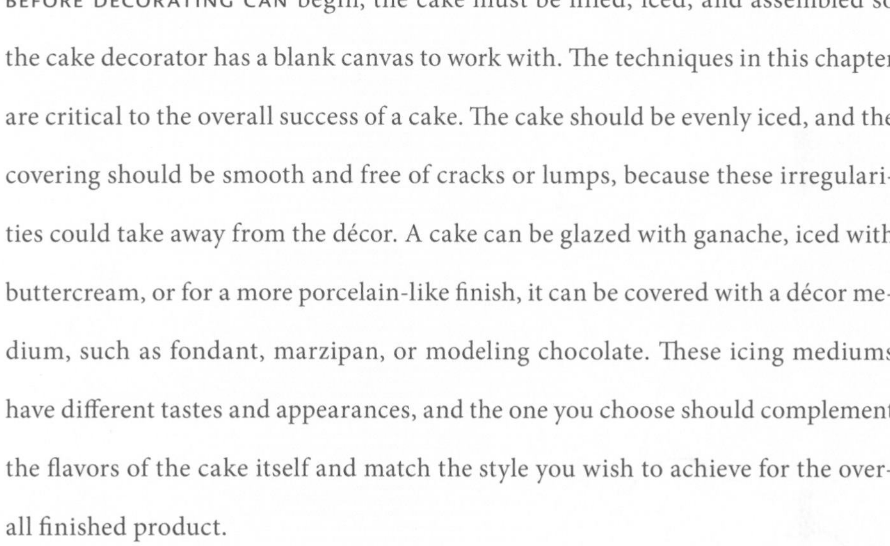

BEFORE DECORATING CAN begin, the cake must be filled, iced, and assembled so the cake decorator has a blank canvas to work with. The techniques in this chapter are critical to the overall success of a cake. The cake should be evenly iced, and the covering should be smooth and free of cracks or lumps, because these irregularities could take away from the décor. A cake can be glazed with ganache, iced with buttercream, or for a more porcelain-like finish, it can be covered with a décor medium, such as fondant, marzipan, or modeling chocolate. These icing mediums have different tastes and appearances, and the one you choose should complement the flavors of the cake itself and match the style you wish to achieve for the overall finished product.

No matter how a cake is to be finished, it must first be masked in buttercream, which is also known as the crumb coat. Using the masking technique, you can use the buttercream to make the sides of the cake straight and the top of the cake flat and even. Another coating of buttercream can finish the cake, or a piece of marzipan, fondant, or modeling chocolate can be rolled out and draped over the masked cake.

Deciding how to display the cake is another important decision for the cake decorator. Glass, porcelain, and silver cake plates are excellent for smaller cakes, and

you can also choose plastic or cardboard cake boards that can be purchased at cake decorating and craft stores. These cake boards can be covered in thinned royal icing or fondant to match the color scheme of the cake.

This chapter includes instructions on how to properly assemble a multi-tiered cake to ensure that it is sturdy and that no structural problems will interfere with your decorating. Very little equipment is needed and, in fact, drinking straws work very well as supports in a multi-tiered cake. If you are decorating for the first time, begin with a single cake and then move up to two-tiered or multi-tiered cakes as you practice and develop your skills.

Covering Cake Boards

Cake boards are available at craft and cake decorating stores and can also be ordered online from cake decorating Web sites (see Shopping Resource, page 195). Cake boards can be purchased to fit any size or style of cake, such as squares, hearts, hexagons, and ovals. They are also available in several thicknesses, including ½, ¼, and 3⁄16 inch. For a multi-tier cake, assemble it on a ½-inch-thick cake board because the weight of the cake needs the additional support. Cake boards are most readily available in only two colors: silver and gold. If these do not match the color or style of your cake design, you can cover the cake board in fondant or royal icing so that it blends perfectly with the cake.

COVERING A CAKE BOARD IN FONDANT

1. Color the fondant to the desired shade with paste or gel food coloring.
2. Spread a very thin layer of shortening, corn syrup, or piping gel on top of the cake board. These products will help secure the fondant to the board, but if you have too thick a layer the fondant will not dry smooth and flat.
3. Dust the work surface with cornstarch and roll out the piece of fondant to ⅛-inch thick. Make sure that the entire piece of fondant is the same thickness or the cake board will look uneven.
4. Dust the surface of the fondant with cornstarch. Roll the piece of fondant around the rolling pin and then unroll the fondant on top of the cake board.
5. Smooth the fondant on top of the cake board with an icing smoother. Remove any bubbles that form with a thin needle or pin.
6. Trim the piece of fondant around the perimeter of the cake board with a sharp knife. Allow the fondant to dry for a minimum of 24 hours.
7. Run a glue stick around the uncovered sides of the cake board and apply a ribbon that is the same thickness as the cake board to cover the sides of the board.

COVERING A CAKE BOARD WITH THIN ROYAL ICING

1. Color a bowl of royal icing to the desired shade with paste or gel food coloring.
2. Stir in cool water until the icing has the consistency of maple syrup. It should run off the spoon fairly easily but should not be so watery that it is translucent.
3. With a small offset spatula, spread the royal icing over the cake board, filling in small sections at a time. You need to work quickly so that the icing does not harden as you try to blend the sections together. Allow the royal icing to dry for 24 hours before assembling the cake.
4. Run a glue stick around the width of the cake board and apply a ribbon that is the same thickness as the cake board to cover the sides of the board.

Assembling a Cake

CUTTING A CAKE

After the cake is removed from the pan and cooled, it is ready to be cut and filled. You decide how thick or thin you want your cake layers; however, the height of your cake will determine how many layers you can create. If you put too much or too little cake batter into the pan, simply adjust the number of cake layers you cut. A cake baked in a 3-inch-deep cake pan will usually yield three ½-inch layers.

1. Place the cake on a turntable.
2. Using a serrated knife, slice off any dome that might have formed during baking so that the top of the cake is a flat and even surface.
3. Hold the knife with one hand and gently place your other hand on top of the cake. Use the knife to create evenly spaced out slice marks on the side of the cake. These marks will guide you as you cut the layers.
4. Insert the knife into the mark that is the closest to the top of the cake. Keeping the knife perfectly straight, turn the cake on the turntable with your free hand so that the knife creates a line all the way around the cake. Be careful to hold the knife level or the cake layer will be thicker on one side of the cake.
5. Continue turning the cake as you hold the knife steady while using a gentle sawing motion inward. The knife will continue slicing the cake all the way to the center.

ABOVE: *Cutting a cake into two equal layers with a serrated knife*

When slicing smaller cakes (6 inches or less): It can be easier when slicing small cakes to run the knife straight through the cake layer in one step. Because of their smaller size, you will find it much easier to cut even cake layers than you would with larger cakes.

ABOVE: *Assembling a cake with equal amounts of filling between each layer. The final layer is placed on top of the filling, then gently pressed into position.*

Filling a Cake

For single-tier cakes, it is often easier to fill and ice the cake on the cake board or platter you wish to serve it on. Any icing or crumbs that fall onto a platter or cake stand can be wiped off with a damp cloth. However, do not fill or ice a cake on a cake board that has been covered in royal icing or fondant, because any crumbs or icing will ruin the covering. The amount of filling you need for each layer depends on the size of the layer itself and how thick you want the filling to be. Italian or Swiss meringue buttercreams are firmer and more stable than lighter fillings, such as mousses and curds. Consequently, you can make a thicker layer of buttercream than you can of curd or mousse, unless they are stabilized with gelatin. However, the layer of filling should be no thicker than the cake layers. When filling cakes, you want to have two separate bowls: one with fresh filling and the other for scraping off your spatula so that crumbs from the cake do not get into your clean filling.

FILLING A SINGLE-TIER CAKE

1. If you are filling the cake on the serving platter, place a small amount of icing onto the platter to secure the base layer to the dish. This will prevent the cake from moving around. If desired, brush the cake layer with a flavored simple syrup. Using a spatula, place a dollop of filling in the center of the cake. Using a small offset spatula for smaller cakes, or a larger offset spatula for cakes over 6 inches, work the filling from the center of the cake to the sides. You want the filling to reach the very edges of the cake.

2. Scrape any excess filling off the spatula. Gently glide the smooth edge of the spatula across the filling to remove any excess and to make the filling smooth and even. You want the layer of filling to be as even as possible, so if you see certain areas that are lower or higher than others, simply add or remove filling until the whole layer is level.

3. Place the second cake layer on top of the filling and press it down gently. Scrape off any filling that pushes out the sides. Fill this layer and repeat until all of the layers are filled and the last cake layer has been placed on top.

FILLING AND STACKING MULTI-TIERED CAKES

The techniques are identical and only the setup changes slightly. When filling larger cakes, it is easier to place the cake on a turntable so that you can hold the spatula completely still at a slight angle and then turn the turntable to smooth and even out the filling layer. In addition, with multi-tiered cakes, you want to fill and cover them on separate, ⅛-inch-thick cake boards and then assemble the entire cake on a clean cake board once all of the tiers are ready. At this point you will only have to add the finishing borders at the base of each cake and any additional décor that ser unify the tiers. Of course the final embellishments or décor to the top tier shoul added as a final step.

To achieve the correct visual proportions when making a multi-tiered cake, you will want to use deeper pans. The diameter is of your choosing, but each of the cakes should be made in pans that are 3 inches deep. Using pans that are the more conventional 1½ or 2 inches deep will produce a cake that has a flattened appearance.

When creating a multi-tiered cake, the weight to be supported by each ascending tier can be significant, making the means of support an important consideration. Wooden dowels or plastic straws should be inserted into each cake before a tier is placed on top. In this way each tier is supported by the straws or dowels rather than the cake below. (See page 57 for more information on doweling a cake.)

Masking and Icing a Cake

Masking is the process of applying a thin layer of buttercream to seal in the crumbs on a cake and create crisp, straight edges for the final coating of icing or fondant to follow. It is also known as the crumb coat. Masking requires a straight spatula (also called a palette knife) to ice the sides of the cake and an offset spatula to ice the top. The layer of buttercream should be quite thin. If it is a vanilla cake you should be able to see the cake through the icing. If you are masking a chocolate cake and want to cover it with white fondant, make sure you cannot see the cake through the buttercream. This way, you know that you will not see the cake through the white fondant. While masking, make sure to scrape your spatula into a separate container so your fresh buttercream does not get crumbs in it. Each tier of a multi-tiered cake must be placed on separate cardboard cake boards before masking. If the cake is not going to be covered with fondant, apply a slightly thicker layer of buttercream so the cake cannot be seen through the icing.

1. Begin by placing the cake on a cardboard cake board the exact size of the cake. If the cake shrank during baking, trace the outline of the cake onto the cake board with a pencil and then cut out the appropriate size round. Place the cake on a turntable.

2. Place a scoop of buttercream on top of the cake you are going to mask. Using the offset spatula, spread and smooth the icing over the surface of the cake. You want the icing to extend over the sides of the cake by about ½ inch. Use the edge of the spatula to remove any excess buttercream and make sure that the top of the cake is level. This is especially important when assembling multi-tiered cakes because if the bottom tier is not level, the cake on top of it will be uneven as well. To determine if

… icing skills, ice … and then gently run … e up the cake, creating long … pattern will hide any irregularities in … icing. Another option is to toast almonds or other nuts and then press the nuts against the sides of the cake to cover the sides.

the cake is even, place a small level (like the ones used in construction) on top of the cake and check to see if the cake is flat or if it is tilting to one side.

3. Next, mask the sides of the cake using the buttercream to build up a ridge that is approximately ½ inch taller than the cake on all sides. This ridge enables the cake decorator to create a crisp top edge around the entire cake. To do this, scoop buttercream onto the end of the straight palette knife and smooth it across a small area of the cake. Continue to apply buttercream to the sides of the cake, smoothing as you go.

4. After you have iced the whole length of one section, step back and examine the side of the cake to make sure the icing is straight and not at an angle. If it is at an angle, add or scrape away buttercream until the side is straight.

5. To create the ridge, place a small amount of buttercream at the end of the straight spatula and apply it to the top lip of the cake. Smooth the sides so that the buttercream is incorporated into the rest of the icing. Do not use too much icing because this will build up the top area of the cake and make it uneven. Create the ridge around the entire perimeter of the cake.

6. Using a small offset spatula, smooth the ridge in a small section at a time. Glide the spatula across the ridge towards the center like a landing airplane. Apply the same amount of pressure each time so the edges of the cake are even. If one area of the rim is lower than the rest of the cake, simply build up another ridge at that area and smooth the edge flat again.

BELOW LEFT: *Begin icing a cake by spreading a layer of icing on the top of the cake that extends slightly over the sides.* CENTER: *Ice the sides of the cake by applying icing with a large, straight palette knife; smooth the sides with the edge of the palette knife.* RIGHT: *Smooth the top of the cake by running an offset palette knife across the rim of icing on the top edge of the cake.*

MASKING A SQUARE OR RECTANGULAR CAKE

The process of masking a square cake is virtually the same as a round cake, however square cakes are a bit more challenging because they have four corners that must be masked to create sharp, straight edges.

1. Place the cake on a turntable. Begin by icing the top of the cake so that it is flat and level. Again, you want about ½ inch of icing to extend over the edge of the cake.
2. Begin masking the sides, building up the ridge as you move across the cake. When you come to a corner, create an edge of buttercream that extends past the end of each side of the corner. Once you have built up the corner, use the sharp edge of the straight spatula to smooth the sides, making sure that they are straight.

COMBING A CAKE

A cake comb is a metal or plastic triangle or square with grooves in the sides that create a design in the icing. When combing a round cake, hold the cake comb still and let the turntable do the work. With a square cake, run the cake comb yourself across each of the cake's four sides.

1. Place the cake on a turntable and ice the cake with buttercream. You do not need to smooth the icing very much.
2. Hold the cake comb against the side of the cake.
3. With one hand holding the cake comb in place, use the other hand to rotate the turntable. Hold the cake comb still and let the cake move across the comb.
4. Continue turning the cake until the design is even across the cake.
5. Smooth the icing on the top of the cake (see Masking and Icing a Cake, beginning on page 51).

ABOVE: *Run the cake comb with equal pressure across the sides of the square cake.*

Covering a Cake with Fondant or Modeling Chocolate

A cake enrobed with fondant or modeling chocolate has a smooth and polished finish, making it an ideal canvas for many cake decorating mediums. To cover a cake with fondant or modeling chocolate, you will need a large work surface; a rolling pin; cornstarch (for fondant), cocoa powder (for dark modeling chocolate), or confectioners' sugar (for white modeling chocolate) in a cheesecloth pouch (see page 38); two fondant smoothers; a thin needle for removing air bubbles; a pizza wheel; and a sharp paring knife. The cake you are covering must chill for at least 1 hour so the buttercream has a chance to harden slightly. If the buttercream is too soft, the cake will become deformed as you try to smooth the décor medium on top of it.

CAKE-COVERING TROUBLESHOOTING

A few problems may arise when covering a cake with fondant or modeling chocolate, but they can all be fixed.

- If fondant becomes too dry (usually because there was too much cornstarch while rolling) it may appear cracked. Gently rub some vegetable shortening into the cracked area to smooth it out.
- If modeling chocolate is handled too much, it will take on an oily appearance. If this occurs, knead in a little cocoa powder (for dark modeling chocolate) or confectioners' sugar (for white modeling chocolate).
- If fondant is rolled too thinly it may split in weak areas as you are smoothing it. To fix this, roll out a piece of fondant to about ⅛-inch thick. Cut a strip that is a bit wider than the split itself. Adhere the piece of fondant to the cake and use a small amount of vegetable shortening to smooth the edges so that it blends with the rest of the fondant.
- Removing too much fondant as you are trimming the base of the cake can be fixed in a similar manner to a split in the fondant. Roll a thin piece of fondant just slightly larger than the area you need to fix. Adhere the piece of fondant to the cake and use vegetable shortening to smooth the edges so that it blends with the rest of the fondant.
- Do not forget that any irregularities can easily be covered with candy, flowers, piping, and other fondant or gum paste decorations. Simply reconfigure your design slightly to cover any undesirable areas of the cake.

TO COVER A ROUND, HEART, OR HEXAGON CAKE:

The following instructions refer to working with fondant; when working with modeling chocolate, substitute cocoa powder (for dark modeling chocolate) or confectioners' sugar (for white modeling chocolate) wherever cornstarch is called for.

1. Lightly dust the work surface with cornstarch. Roll the quantity of fondant needed for the size of the cake into a circle ⅛-inch thick. Frequently turn the fondant and dust additional cornstarch on top and underneath to prevent it from sticking to the work surface or to the rolling pin.
2. Lightly dust the surface of the fondant with cornstarch and starting at one end, roll it up with the rolling pin. Lift the rolling pin by its handles and carefully unroll the piece of fondant over the cake, leaving equal amounts of fondant on all sides of the cake.
3. Using a cake smoother, begin smoothing the top of the cake first, gently pushing any air bubbles out the sides of the cake.
4. Once the top is smooth, begin pressing the fondant against the sides of the cake, starting at the top of the cake and then working down. Make sure to use only the palm of your hands as you smooth the sides, because fingers and fingernails will mark the soft fondant.
5. Once the fondant is adhered to the sides of the cake, lightly dust the cake smoothers with cornstarch. With one in each hand, smooth the sides and top of the cake applying a fair amount of pressure. You do not have to be too gentle because the buttercream underneath the fondant is well chilled. This process should remove any marks or lines in the fondant. If at any point the cake smoothers begin to stick to the fondant, apply more cornstarch to the smoothers or sprinkle cornstarch directly on the cake itself.
6. Using a pizza wheel or sharp paring knife, trim the excess fondant leaving about half an inch of fondant around the base of the cake. Place the fondant in an airtight bag so that it can be reused.
7. Next, use the paring knife to trim the fondant so that it is flush with the base of the cake. Smooth the base of the cake with the cake smoothers.
8. The final step is to remove any air bubbles that may form in the fondant. If you find an air pocket, simply puncture it with a thin pin or needle and then smooth the area flat with either the palm of your hand or a cake smoother. Don't be alarmed if there are several air bubbles on your cake because this can be quite common, especially when decorating in the warm summer months. It is also possible for air pockets to form after you've finished covering the cake, so check on the condition of your cake periodically.

9. Wrap the covered cake in plastic wrap and place it in the refrigerator. This will reduce the chances of the cake "sweating" (when condensation forms on the cake).

10. Allow the cake to come to room temperature before peeling off the plastic wrap. This way, the condensation will form on the plastic wrap and not on the cake.

TO COVER A SQUARE OR RECTANGULAR CAKE

The process is identical; however, it is easier to roll the fondant into the shape of the cake you wish to cover. Instead of a circle, roll the fondant into a square larger than the size of the square cake you are going to cover. The fondant should be rolled into a rectangle to cover a rectangular cake.

Lightly dust the work surface with cornstarch. Roll the fondant to approximately ⅛-inch thick. Frequently turn the fondant and dust additional cornstarch on top and underneath the fondant so that it does not stick to the work surface or to the rolling pin.

BELOW LEFT: *Roll the sheet of fondant up with the rolling pin and drape it over the masked cake; ensure that there is enough fondant on all sides of the cake to cover it completely.* **CENTER:** *Smooth the fondant over the cake with the palms of your hands or with a fondant smoother; try to push out all air pockets that may form under the fondant as you smooth it.* **RIGHT:** *Once the excess fondant has been trimmed from the cake, smooth it over one final time with a fondant smoother to ensure that the surface is even.*

Glazing a Cake With Ganache

Keep in mind a cake's height when you are ready to glaze. A shorter cake will need less ganache to cover the top and sides than a taller cake. The ganache should feel slightly warm to the touch, between 100°F and 110°F, for glazing. This temperature ensures that the ganache will be fluid enough to flow over the cake, but it will not lose its shine or melt the buttercream coating underneath.

1. Place the cake on a cardboard circle that is the exact size of the cake. If necessary, trim the cake circle to fit the cake.
2. Place an inverted cake pan, or a similar object that is slightly smaller than the cake itself, on a baking sheet. Position the cake on top of the inverted pan.
3. Prepare a hard ganache (see page 30 for ganache recipe). Once all the chocolate has melted into the cream, allow the ganache to cool to between 100°F and 110°F.
4. Using a ladle or a 1-cup measure, pour 2 cups of chocolate ganache onto the center of the cake; 2 cups is enough to cover a short 6-inch cake. When covering larger cakes, it is better to use more ganache than you think you will need because excess ganache will drip onto the baking sheet and can be reused.
5. Using a large offset palette knife, push the ganache from the center of the cake over the sides. Make sure the top of the cake has a thin and even coating.
6. If the ganache does not cover all of the sides of the cake, use a small knife or offset palette knife to spread some ganache onto those areas.
7. Allow the ganache to drip off of the cake onto the baking sheet. Once the ganache has set, hold the cake from the bottom (remember, there is a cake board that you can hold onto) and trim any excess ganache with a small offset palette knife.

BELOW LEFT: Pour the ganache onto the center of the cake that has been raised off of a glazing screen or cooling rack. CENTER: Coax the ganache over the sides of the cake with an offset palette knife beginning at the center; if necessary, dab extra ganache onto bare areas with a small palette knife. RIGHT: Once the ganache has set, lift the cake off of the glazing screen or cooling rack and trim any excess ganache from the base with a small offset palette knife.

Doweling a Cake

Dowels are to multi-tiered cakes what steel beams are to skyscrapers. Without some sort of support, the weight of the upper tiers will cause them to sink into the tiers below. However, this can be easily avoided by inserting simple drinking straws or wooden dowels for support. The number of supports needed will depend on how large the cake is and how many tiers it must support.

1. Begin with the cake that is to be the bottom tier. Center a cake pan that is the same size as the tier that will go on top of it. Press the pan down gently to make an imprint in the buttercream or fondant. Remove the cake pan. The pan outline will guide the location of the straws.
2. Insert a straw or dowel into the center of the cake, making sure it goes all the way down to the cake board. Use a marker to indicate on the support where it is flush with the top of the cake. Remove the support and wipe off any cake or icing.
3. Cut the support with a pair of scissors or an X-acto knife, using the line as a guide.
4. Use the cut support as a guide to cut the other straws to the same height.
5. Insert the supports into the cake, spacing them out evenly and leaving approximately 1 inch of space between the edge of the cake pan imprint and the supports.
6. To make sure that the next tier will sit evenly on the first tier, place a cake board the same size as the next tier on top of the supports and then place a leveler on top of the board. If a cake has high and low areas (is not even), adjust the heights of the supports so the next tier will be level. The supports in short areas will have to be slightly higher than the cake so that the next tier will not be slanted.
7. Insert supports into all the cakes except for the top tier.

ASSEMBLING MULTI-TIERED CAKES

The most challenging part of assembling a cake is centering the tiers. Use the supports and imprint from the cake pans as guides. If adjustment is necessary, use the palm of your hand to push the cake in the direction it must go to be centered.

1. Pipe a small amount of royal icing on top of each support.
2. Using a large offset spatula, lift the next tier and brace the cake by holding the cake board.
3. Position the cake on top of the tier below so that it is perfectly centered. Use the supports as a guide. Place one end of the cake down onto the supports and then slowly remove the spatula and your fingers until the entire cake is correctly positioned on the tier beneath. Repeat with the remaining cake tiers.

Piping

PIPING IS AN extremely versatile technique in cake decorating. Not only are there a variety of icing mediums to choose from, such as buttercream, meringue, ganache, and piping gel, but there also is an endless array of borders, flowers, designs, and messages that can be created by piping. The technique of piping, however, is not limited to icing mediums.

Tempered chocolate or melted coating chocolate also can be piped into shapes and designs. Once they have set, these décor pieces can be removed carefully and secured onto the cake with icing or more chocolate. Small chocolate pieces make attractive borders, and several pieces can be put together to make a three-dimensional figure, such as a butterfly. Chocolate can also be piped directly onto a cake to create a message or a design.

An entire cake can be decorated with piped decorations, flowers, leaves, and borders. Piping a personalized message on a fondant or chocolate plaque will make a cake meaningful and special. Piping can also be combined with several other décor techniques, such as stamping, painting, and embossing, to create an impressive presentation.

This chapter provides you with the basic techniques on how to prepare, fill, and hold a piping bag. In addition to the traditional cloth or plastic piping bags, this chapter explains how to make disposable piping bags out of parchment paper. This

allows you to make a pastry bag whenever you need one and gives you more control over the size of the bag. This chapter also describes the variety of piping tips, and which ones are needed to create specific flowers, borders, and designs.

Making a Paper Cornet for Piping

For piping writing and decorations onto cakes, a parchment cornet works extremely well and allows control over the size of the opening.

1. Cut a rectangle of parchment in half diagonally to form 2 triangles. An 8- × 10-inch rectangle will make a manageable size piping cornet, however a smaller or larger piece of parchment can be used depending on the project.

2. Hold the triangle at its 90-degree corner with one hand, with the long side away from you. With your other hand hold the point of the short side and curl it inward until the 2 points meet and a cone shape is formed.

3. Hold the 2 points together with one hand while the other takes the last point and wraps it around the cone until all points are together. While maintaining the cone shape, fold all points into the cornet, and make a crease so it will not unravel.

BELOW LEFT: Cut a triangle out of parchment paper to the desired size; for delicate garnishes a small cornet is best. Hold the 90° angle of the triangle with the long end facing outward; fold the angle pointing away from you into a small cone whose point meets the center point of the triangle. CENTER: Fold the bottom end around the first cone. RIGHT: Fold the flap into the cone; the cornet is ready to be filled with chocolate, icing, or piping gel.

4. Place the chocolate or icing gently in the cornet (no more then half full) and secure the top by bringing the sides together and folding the flap into the cone.

Filling a Piping Bag With Icing

Fill a piping bag no more than one-half full. A heavy bag of icing is difficult to hold and might make your hand hurt after extended use. Also, overfilling the piping bag may result in icing shooting out the back of the bag instead of through the tip. Use the following method to properly fill a piping bag with icing:

1. Place the coupler inside of the piping bag and then place the tip on top of the coupler. Secure the tip to the coupler with the screw piece.

2. Fold the bag halfway over so that it forms a large opening. Use a spatula to scoop the icing into the opening. The bag should be filled about halfway.

3. Lift the sides of the bag back up and push the icing down towards the tip. Pinch the top of the bag together where the icing ends, twisting it around tightly to secure the top. Tightly wrap an elastic band around the top of the bag. This will prevent icing from coming out the top of the bag.

BELOW LEFT: *Fold the bag halfway over so it forms a large opening; use a spatula to scoop the icing into the opening; the bag should be filled about halfway.* RIGHT: *Use your dominant hand to hold the bag at the sealed end, wrapping your fingers and thumb around the bag itself; if needed, brace the bag at the tip to give you more control while piping.*

Holding a Piping Bag

Whether you are piping with buttercream, royal icing, ganache, or gel, there are simple techniques that will give you greater control over your design.

1. Do not fill the bag more than halfway full. The lighter the bag, the easier it will be to hold and pipe with.

2. Use your dominant hand to hold the bag at the sealed end, wrapping your fingers and thumb around the bag itself. If needed, brace the bag at the tip to give you more control while piping.

3. While piping, always apply gentle pressure from the top of the bag and not from the middle or the bottom.

4. When you are not using your piping bag, place a damp paper towel over the tip so that the icing does not dry inside.

OPPOSITE: *Piping tips, clockwise from upper left: A plain tip is used for piping inscriptions, dots, and pearl borders. A rose tip creates flowers and decorative swags. Star tips pipe stars of various sizes. Leaf tips create various shaped leaves, vines, and decorative swags. A basket tip creates a basket weave pattern. An open star tip creates shell borders and swags. Star tips are commonly used to decoratively pipe icing and ganache onto cakes or cupcakes.*

Happy

Coloring Icing

Liquid, paste, and powdered food colorings are best suited for coloring certain icings. Liquid food coloring can change the consistency of royal icing if too much is used. However, they are very strong and usually only a dot or two of liquid food coloring is needed to color a whole batch of icing. Paste food colors will not change the consistency of royal icing or buttercream, but too much paste color will make fondant too sticky to work with. A small amount of liquid or paste color is generally all that is needed to color a batch of fondant. Start by coloring a small piece of fondant a darker color than what you want the final product to look like. Knead the small piece of colored fondant into the larger piece of uncolored fondant until it is evenly distributed. If it is too dark, knead in more white fondant. If it is too light, color another small piece of the fondant slightly darker and knead that piece into the larger piece. Powdered food colors will not change the consistency of icing or sugar paste, but the food color has to be thoroughly incorporated into the icing medium so that there are no little dots of powdered color.

Piping a Rose With Buttercream

Piping bag fitted with a coupler
#5 plain tip
Rose tip
Rose nail
Parchment paper
Buttercream
Small offset palette knife

NOTE: Roses and flowers can also be piped directly onto the cake, thus eliminating the time to chill the flower.

The same technique applies to piping a rose with royal icing or meringue.

1. Fit a piping bag with a coupler and a #5 plain tip. Fill the bag halfway with buttercream.
2. Place a dot of icing in the center of a rose nail. Press a square of parchment or wax paper on top of the icing.
3. Pipe the flower center with a plain tip. Hold the piping bag at a 90-degree angle to the rose nail. Apply pressure to the top of the piping bag and allow the cone to build up as you gradually raise the piping bag. Once it is about 1-inch tall, stop applying pressure and pull the tip away from the center.
4. Remove the plain tip and attach the rose tip to the piping bag.
5. To form the first inner petal, hold the piping bag with the wide end of the tip on the center cone and the thin end pointing slightly inward. Apply gentle pressure and turn the nail clockwise, holding the piping bag in the same position. A ribbon of icing will surround the central cone.
6. To create the first row of three petals, hold the piping bag so that the wide end of the tip is at the base of the inner petal and the thin end is pointing straight up. Apply pressure and move the bag up slightly, around the central petal, and then back

down, turning the rose nail counterclockwise one-third of a turn at the same time. Pipe two more petals in the same manner. Begin each petal at the center of the previous petal so that they appear to be overlapping.

7. As you build up the rose, pipe each layer of petals slightly lower down than the previous layer, holding the piping bag a little less vertically as you apply each new layer of petals. This will give the rose a more realistic appearance. Each new layer of petals should have an uneven number of petals so that the rose does not appear square.

8. Once the rose is piped, gently remove the piece of parchment from the rose nail with a small offset palette knife.

9. Place the rose in the refrigerator so that it will harden slightly. This makes the rose easier to remove from the parchment with an offset palette knife so that it can be placed on the cake.

BELOW LEFT: *Pipe the 1-inch tall flower center with a #5 plain tip by holding the bag at a 90-degree angle to the rose nail and applying pressure as you gradually raise the piping bag.* CENTER: *To create the petals, hold the piping bag so that the wide end of the tip is at the base of the inner petal and the thin end is pointing straight up; apply pressure and move the bag up slightly, around the central petal, and then back down, turning the rose nail counterclockwise one-third of a turn at the same time.* RIGHT: *Pipe three, slightly overlapping petals at each layer; as you build up the rose, pipe each layer of petals slightly lower down than the previous layer.*

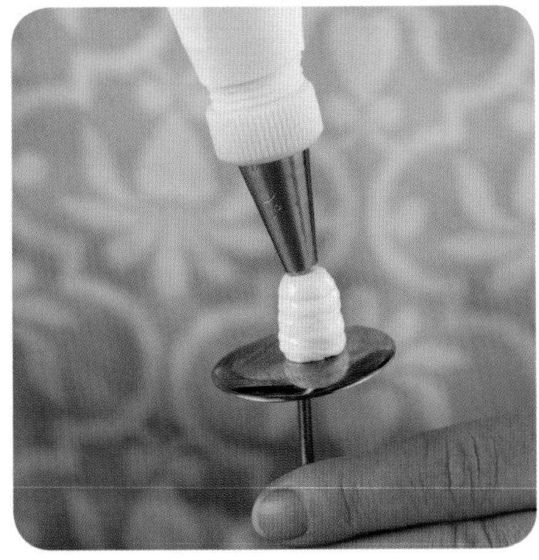

Piping Mums With Buttercream

Piping bag fitted with a coupler

Rose tip

Buttercream

NOTE: To achieve the two-color icing effect shown below, dip a small paint brush in the paste color of your choice and apply a stripe of color up the inside of the piping bag. Fill the bag with white or another color buttercream to produce the two-color effect.

1. Fill a pastry bag fitted with a rose tip approximately two-thirds full with buttercream.
2. Begin by holding the rose tip flat against the cake or cupcake with the thin part of the tip facing out.
3. Apply gentle pressure and move the piping bag in a half-circle motion to create the first petal. Repeat until the first row of petals has been piped.
4. For the next layer of petals, increase the angle slightly so that the tip is not as flat against the cake as the previous row. Pipe a row of petals that are slightly shorter than the previous row. This way each row will be distinct.
5. Continue piping additional rows of petals, increasing the angle of the tip to the surface of the cake or cupcake a little more with each new row.

Piping a Begonia With Buttercream

Piping bag fitted with a coupler

Rose tip

Buttercream

1. Fill a pastry bag fitted with a rose tip approximately two-thirds full with buttercream.
2. Hold the bag so that the tip is sitting straight up on the cake or cupcake with the thin part of the rose tip facing up.
3. Apply gentle pressure and move the piping bag in a back-and-forth motion to create the first petal. Repeat until the first row of petals has been piped.
4. If desired, pipe another row of petals on top of the first. Hold the bag at the same angle and pipe slightly shorter petals in between the petals on the first layer.

__LEFT:__ Holding the tip straight up on the cake and moving your hand in a back-and-forth motion while applying gentle pressure will create the tall and thin petals of a mum. __RIGHT:__ Holding the tip flat against the cake and moving your hand in a circular motion as you apply gentle pressure will create the round petals of a begonia.

Piping Vines and Leaves With Buttercream, Royal Icing, Meringue, or Ganache

Piping bag fitted with a coupler

Leaf tip

Royal icing, buttercream, Swiss meringue, or ganache

Vines and leaves are very easy to pipe and do not require a perfectly steady hand. Vines are piped with plain tips (circular opening), and the tip opening determines the thickness of the vines. A #2 tip will create thin, delicate vines; a #4 or #5 tip will create thick vines, which would be ideal for a jungle- or forest-themed cake.

To pipe vines, prepare a piping bag with either buttercream or royal icing and apply gentle pressure as you move the piping bag across the cake, mimicking the irregular patterns vines make in nature.

For piping leaves, leaf tips, with their V-shaped openings, come in a variety of sizes, and a leaf tip is usually included in piping tip sets. The most commonly used leaf tips are numbers 65, 67, and 352. Prepare a bag fitted with a leaf tip with buttercream, royal icing, Italian or Swiss meringue, or ganache.

1. When you pipe a leaf, you are actually creating the base of the leaf first, so position the bag on an area of the cake where you want the leaf to start.
2. Apply gentle pressure until a small bulb forms and then pull the tip outward.
3. Once the leaf is the length you want it, release the pressure and pull the tip up sharply to create the leaf's pointed end.

NOTE: If you are piping with royal icing and it is not pulling out to a perfect pointed tip and is breaking, the icing may be too stiff and can be softened slightly with a small amount of water. If you are having the same difficulty with buttercream, stir a small amount by hand with a spatula to smooth it out.

Pearl Dot Border

Piping bag fitted with a coupler

Plain tip

Royal icing, buttercream, Swiss meringue, or ganache

The pearl dot is a very simple border, and it gives a cake a polished finish. A small pearl dot is very elegant, whereas larger dots are more suited for a fun child's cake. The size of the pearl dot is determined by the size of the piping tip you use. A small pearl dot needs a #2 tip, whereas a larger border needs a #4 tip or higher.

1. Prepare a piping bag with the appropriate-sized tip. Fill the bag between half to two-thirds full with buttercream or royal icing. Secure the end of the bag with an elastic band so that no icing comes out the end of the bag.
2. Hold the bag at a 45-degree angle to the base of the cake. Hold the bag steady and apply a small amount of pressure to the top of the bag. Move the bag up slightly to give the icing space to create a round ball. Release the pressure, and in one motion, pull the tip to the right of the dot and downward (to the left of the dot if you're left-handed).
3. Repeat this process all the way around the base of the cake. Try to apply the same amount of pressure for each dot so that they are the same size.

Piping a large pearl using a large plain tip such as a #8 can be used to ice cupcakes. The "large pearl" can then be left as is, can have any number of décor elements added to it, or can be spread or textured to create different effects.

NOTE: The pearl dot border takes a bit of practice to perfect. Try practicing your piping on a Styrofoam cake dummy or a cardboard box.

Meringue Décor

Piping bag fitted with a coupler

Appropriate tip (see following instructions)

Swiss or Italian meringue

Baking sheet

Parchment paper or a nonstick baking mat

Meringue is a décor medium that is both delicious and easy to work with. It can be piped into flowers, leaves, letters, numbers, animals, and many other images. Placing a design underneath a piece of parchment enables you to trace a design with a meringue. Meringue is piped in a similar manner to buttercream or royal icing and the piping bag should be held in the same manner as you would with a piping bag filled with these icings (see page 61–65 for piping techniques). However, because Swiss meringue is lighter than icing, you can use a larger piping bag and tips than you would with buttercream or royal icing. Fill the bag halfway full so that no meringue comes out the top of the piping bag.

Piping Meringue Flowers

See page 69 for drying instructions.

1. To prepare meringue decorations, fill a large piping bag about two-thirds full of Swiss meringue. Secure the top so that no meringue comes out while you are piping.
2. Pipe a large dot of meringue on all four corners of a baking sheet and press a piece of parchment down on top. This will prevent the parchment from moving while you are piping the flowers and while they are drying in the oven.
3. To pipe letters or numbers, use a large plain or star tip, such as a #6 or larger. Pipe the design either freehand or trace an image that is placed underneath the parchment before the parchment is secured to the baking sheet with meringue.
4. To make daisies, use a #2 tip to pipe approximately six thin petals of equal size with a dot for the center of each flower. The size of the flower will depend on the size of the cake or cupcake you are decorating.

LEFT: *Pipe a mound of Swiss meringue on top of each cupcake; to create the spikes, press the back of a spoon against the meringue and then pull up sharply.* RIGHT: *Use a small kitchen torch to lightly caramelize the meringue; the broiler of an oven can also brown the meringue, but the cupcakes have to be watched carefully.*

5. To make mums, you need a #5 plain tip, a #81 tip, a rose nail, and a small square of parchment secured to the nail with a dot of meringue. Holding the bag at a 90-degree angle to the parchment, pipe a mound ¼-inch high with the #5 tip. Switch to the #81 tip to pipe the petals. Hold the bag at a 45-degree angle to the edge of the center you just piped. The half-moon shaped opening of the tip should face upward. Apply pressure to create a ½-inch-long, cupped petal. Pull the tip up after you have stopped applying pressure to release the icing. Create a row of base petals. Repeat this technique on the second row, making the petal slightly shorter and piping them in between the petals on the first row. Continue piping rows of petals, making the petals shorter than the previous row. Transfer the mum to a baking sheet for drying. Secure the piece of parchment to the baking sheet with a dot of meringue.

6. To pipe the roses for the Meringue Flowers Cake, fill a piping bag with meringue that has been fitted with a rose tip. Secure a square of wax paper or parchment to the nail with a small amount of meringue. Holding the tip with the thin portion facing upwards, apply pressure to the top of the piping bag and turn the piping nail, thereby creating a center with layers of "petals" around it. When the rose is of the desired size, stop turning the nail and pull the piping tip away sharply. Transfer the rose to a parchment-lined baking sheet with a small offset palette knife for drying.

7. To pipe meringue cigarettes, fit a piping bag with a #7 or #10 tip. Pipe the meringue in long, straight rows on a baking sheet lined with either parchment paper or a nonstick baking mat. Once dry, meringue cigarettes can be garnishes for a cake or they can be cut to the height of the cake and arranged around the outside.

DRYING MERINGUE DÉCOR

1. Preheat the oven to 200°F.
2. Place the baking sheet with the meringue designs into the oven, ensuring that the corners of the parchment paper have been secured to the baking sheet with meringue.
3. Turn off the oven and allow the meringue to dry. The length of the drying time depends on the thickness of the meringue décor. A thin daisy will dry faster than a thick rose or mum.
4. Remove the meringue designs from the oven and allow them to cool completely.
5. Once the meringue designs have cooled, loosen the parchment paper from the sheet tray and loosen the décor from the parchment with a small offset spatula. Place the designs on a parchment-lined sheet tray.
6. Store the meringue designs in an airtight container in a cool, dry place.

Piping Chocolate Décor

Many designs can be piped with either tempered or melted coating chocolate, which contains vegetable fats and sets without tempering. Tempered chocolate can be piped directly onto a cake or fondant plaque. A design can also be piped onto acetate; once it sets, it can be carefully removed and placed on the cake. For more intricate designs, place the image you want to create beneath the acetate and trace the design with the tempered chocolate.

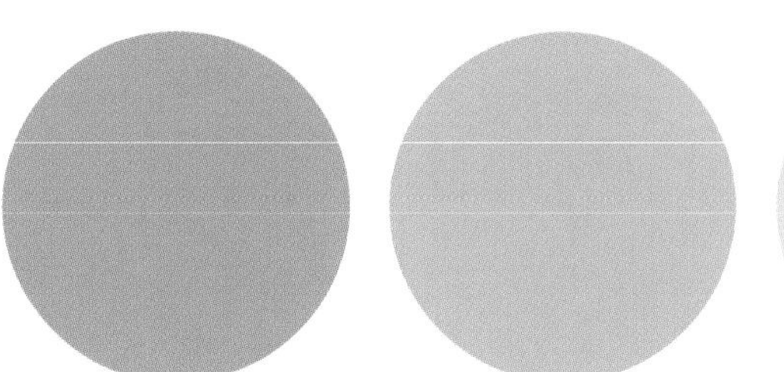

Floodwork

This technique requires two types of royal icing: a pastry bag filled with firm royal icing of the desired color and a piping bag of lightly watered down royal icing of the same color. The thin icing should have the consistency of whipping cream. Always color the icing before watering it down so that it will not become too thin.

1. If using a stencil or a printed image, place it underneath a piece of acetate or clear plastic, such as a page protector.
2. Using the piping bag of firm royal icing with a small tip, usually a #1, pipe the outline of the image you wish to create. Make sure all the edges meet and the outline forms a sealed barrier for the thinned icing.
3. Immediately fill in the center of the image with the thin royal icing. Apply a small amount of pressure to the top of the piping bag with the thinned icing and move the bag back and forth until the image is filled in. Use the tip of the piping bag to gently push the icing into the corners. You will need a #1 tip for smaller pieces and a #2 tip for larger pieces. If you work quickly, the thinned icing should blend perfectly with the piped outline.
4. Small pieces of floodwork must dry for at least 24 hours and larger pieces will need approximately 2 days. Once the floodwork is completely dry, carefully loosen the edges and remove the piece with a small offset spatula.
5. Pipe firm royal icing onto the back of the floodwork piece in order to secure it onto the cake.

BELOW LEFT: *After creating an outline of a design with icing, dark piping gel or chocolate, fill in each section with colored piping gel.* **CENTER:** *After filling a paper cornet one-half full with piping gel, cut out a small opening with a pair of scissors, and pipe designs or filigree onto a cake or plaque.* **RIGHT:** *After filling a paper cornet half-full with piping gel, cut out a small opening with a pair of scissors, and pipe an inscription onto a dry fondant or chocolate plaque.*

Projects

Buttercream Roses Cake

PREPARATION TIMELINE

- **UP TO 2 DAYS IN ADVANCE:** Cover cake board in fondant if not using a cake plate
- **UP TO 2 DAYS IN ADVANCE:** Bake cake
- **UP TO 2 DAYS IN ADVANCE:** Fill and ice cake with buttercream
- **DAY OF EVENT:** Prepare buttercream roses
- **DAY OF EVENT:** Decorate cake with buttercream roses, buds, wisteria, and leaves

OPPOSITE: *A buttercream covered cake with buttercream roses, wisteria, and leaves and a piped buttercream pearl border*

Components

One 8-inch cake, filled and iced with pale yellow buttercream

12–13 pink and pale yellow buttercream roses (see Piping a Rose, pages 64–65, for method)

15 pink buttercream buds (see Piping a Rose, pages 64–65, for method)

Buttercream leaves (see Piping Vines and Leaves, page 67, for method)

Purple buttercream wisteria

Pale yellow buttercream pearl dot border

Equipment and Materials

CAKE ASSEMBLY

Regular and offset palette knives for icing the cake

Pale yellow buttercream

Cake comb

Turntable

BUTTERCREAM ROSES AND BUDS

Piping bag fitted with a coupler

#5 plain tip

Rose tip

Rose nail

Parchment paper

Pink and pale yellow buttercream

Small offset palette knife

BUTTERCREAM LEAVES

Piping bag fitted with a coupler and a leaf tip

Green buttercream

BUTTERCREAM WISTERIA

Piping bag fitted with a coupler and a small V-tip

Purple buttercream

BUTTERCREAM PEARL DOT BORDER

Piping bag fitted with a coupler and a #5 plain tip

Pale yellow buttercream

VARIATIONS:

Various types of flowers can be piped with buttercream, such as mums and daisies.

CAKE ASSEMBLY

1. Begin by icing the cake with the buttercream. The technique is the same as for masking a cake; however, you will use more buttercream so that no parts of the cake can be seen (see pages 51–53 for icing techniques). Use more buttercream than usual on this cake because it is going to be combed.

2. Holding the cake comb still against the side of the cake, move the turntable quickly. Once the comb has gone around the entire cake, pull it away sharply. This will create a design in the buttercream.

FINISHING

1. Attach a piece of parchment to the rose nail with a small amount of buttercream. Pipe a rose or a bud. Repeat this process with the remaining roses and buds.

2. Pipe the wisteria so that it runs down the sides of the cake. The technique for piping wisteria is the same for piping leaves. Pipe the wisteria closely together so that they appear to be connected on a vine.

3. Transfer the roses to the cake with a small offset palette knife.

4. Pipe leaves around the roses.

5. Pipe a small pearl dot border around the base of the cake.

SERVES 10 TO 12

Meringue Flowers Cake

Components

One 8-inch round cake, filled and iced with buttercream

25–30 meringue roses and buds (see Piping Meringue Flowers, pages 68–69, for method)

Buttercream leaves (see Piping Vines and Leaves, page 67, for method)

Buttercream shell border

White buttercream inscription

Equipment and Materials

CAKE ASSEMBLY

Regular and offset palette knives for icing the cake

Pale orange buttercream

MERINGUE ROSES AND BUDS

Piping bag fitted with a coupler and a rose tip

Swiss meringue

Rose nail

Parchment paper

Small offset palette knife

BUTTERCREAM LEAVES

Piping bag fitted with a coupler and a leaf tip

Green buttercream

SHELL BORDER

Piping bag fitted with a coupler and a medium-sized star tip

Green buttercream

INSCRIPTION

Piping bag fitted with a coupler and a #2 tip

White buttercream or piping gel

PREPARATION TIMELINE

➡ **UP TO 2 DAYS IN ADVANCE:** Cover cake board in fondant if not using a cake plate

➡ **UP TO 2 DAYS IN ADVANCE:** Prepare meringue roses and buds

➡ **UP TO 2 DAYS IN ADVANCE:** Bake cake

➡ **UP TO 2 DAYS IN ADVANCE:** Fill and ice cake with buttercream

➡ **UP TO 1 DAY IN ADVANCE OR DAY OF EVENT:** Decorate cake

OVERLEAF: *A buttercream-covered cake with meringue roses, buttercream leaves, a piped buttercream inscription, and a buttercream shell border*

CAKE ASSEMBLY

1. Ice the cake with pale orange buttercream. The technique is the same as for masking a cake; however you will use more buttercream so that no parts of the cake can be seen (see pages 51-53 for icing techniques).

FINISHING

1. Pipe the meringue roses and buds and dry them in the oven (see Drying Meringue Décor, page 69).
2. Pipe the shell border around the upper rim and the base of the cake with buttercream.
3. Transfer the meringue flowers to the cake with a small offset palette knife, and secure with additional buttercream.
4. Pipe leaves around the meringue roses with buttercream.

VARIATIONS:

If you don't want to use meringue, buttercream, ganache, or royal icing can be used to make the roses or another type of flower. If you aren't confident in your piping skills, roses can be shaped out of marzipan, modeling chocolate, gum paste, or fondant.

MAKES 24 CUPCAKES

Buttercream Flowers Cupcakes

PREPARATION TIMELINE

- **UP TO 2 DAYS IN ADVANCE:** Bake cupcakes
- **DAY OF EVENT:** Decorate cupcakes

Components

Cupcakes

Equipment and Materials

Buttercream

Liquid or gel food colors

Piping bag fitted with a coupler

Rose tip

Leaf tip (optional)

FINISHING

1. Color the buttercream various shades for the flowers.
2. Ice the cupcakes. The icing can be piped onto the cupcakes in a design or spread over the cupcakes with a small palette knife. Use the rose tip to pipe roses, mums or other flowers onto each cupcake (see Piping a Rose with Buttercream, page 64–65 and Piping Mums with Buttercream, page 66).

OPPOSITE: *Chocolate cupcakes with variegated buttercream flowers*

MAKES 24 CUPCAKES

Chocolate Bug Cupcakes

PREPARATION TIMELINE

- **UP TO 1 WEEK IN ADVANCE:** Make the chocolate bugs
- **UP TO 2 DAYS IN ADVANCE:** Make the cupcakes
- **DAY OF EVENT:** Decorate the cupcakes

Components

Chocolate cupcakes

Chocolate butterflies, ants, and spiders (see Piping Chocolate Décor, page 69, for method)

Equipment and Materials

Tempered dark chocolate or coating chocolate

Green buttercream

Piping bag with a large leaf tip

Acetate or a page protector

Paper cornets

Butterfly, ant, and spider patterns (see Templates, page 196)

FINISHING

1. Pipe large leaves with the green buttercream on top of each cupcake.
2. Begin each insect by placing the body piece in the center of the cupcake. For a butterfly, insert the wings into the buttercream next to the body at an angle. For a spider, insert the legs into the buttercream right next to the body so that they appear to be connected.

OPPOSITE: *Piped coating chocolate comes to life in these three-dimensional insects. The bodies and legs or wings are piped separately on parchment paper and then assembled on the cupcakes once the chocolate has set.*

MAKES 24 CUPCAKES

Lemon Meringue Cupcakes

PREPARATION TIMELINE

- UP TO 2 DAYS IN ADVANCE: Make the cupcakes
- UP TO 2 DAYS IN ADVANCE: Make the lemon curd
- DAY OF EVENT: Make the Swiss meringue topping
- DAY OF EVENT: Decorate the cupcakes

Components

Lemon Chiffon cupcakes (see page 18 for recipe)

Lemon Curd (see page 29 for recipe)

Swiss Meringue (see page 33 for recipe)

Equipment and Materials

Piping bag fitted with a coupler

Large tip for filling

Large plain tip for piping meringue

Kitchen torch or an oven broiler

FINISHING

1. Fill the piping bag two-thirds full with lemon curd.
2. Insert the tip as far as it will go inside the center of the cupcake and apply gentle pressure. Try not to squeeze too hard or lemon curd will squirt out the top of the cupcake. Stop filling once you see any lemon curd around the base of the tip. Repeat with the remaining cupcakes.
3. Clean the piping bag and fill it two-thirds full with Swiss meringue. Pipe a large pearl of meringue on top of each cupcake.
4. Use the back of a spoon to lift up areas of the meringue, creating spikes.
5. Lightly toast the meringue with a kitchen torch or under the broiler until the tips of the meringue are golden brown (see page 68 for meringue topping instructions).

OPPOSITE: *A lemon chiffon cupcake filled with lemon curd and topped with toasted Swiss meringue*

MAKES 24 CUPCAKES

Sugar Marshmallow Cupcakes

PREPARATION TIMELINE

➡ UP TO 2 DAYS IN ADVANCE:
Make the cupcakes

➡ DAY OF EVENT:
Decorate the cupcakes

Components

Cupcakes

Sugar marshmallows (see Marshmallow Flowers and Designs for Cupcakes, page 104)

Equipment and Materials

Buttercream, ganache, or meringue for icing

Large marshmallows

Scissors

Sanding sugar or colored nonpareils

Powdered food color (for coloring the sanding sugar)

Gum drops for the flower centers

Small palette knife

FINISHING

1. Ice the cupcakes. The icing can be piped onto the cupcakes into a design or it can be spread over the cupcake with a small palette knife.

2. Prepare the sugar marshmallows and arrange them on top of the cupcakes to resemble flowers and other designs.

OPPOSITE: *Gum drop centers and marshmallow slices dipped in colored sanding sugar or colorful nonpareils form the flowers on these very child-friendly cupcakes.*

SERVES 28 TO 32

Paint-by-Number Cake

Components

One 11 × 15-inch rectangular cake, filled and iced with buttercream

White fondant plaque (see page 127 for method)

Paint-by-number design of your choice (see Finishing, page 88)

Buttercream shell border

Equipment and Materials

CAKE ASSEMBLY

Large offset palette knife for icing the cake

White buttercream

FONDANT PLAQUE

1 pound white fondant

Cornstarch

Rolling pin

Knife

PAINT-BY-NUMBER DESIGN

Piping bag filled with black piping gel (#2 tip)

Piping bags filled with different colored piping gel (#5 tip)

Food-color markers

BUTTERCREAM SHELL BORDER

Buttercream of desired color

Shell tip

Piping bag

PREPARATION TIMELINE

➡ **UP TO 2 DAYS IN ADVANCE:** Cover cake board in fondant if not using a cake plate

➡ **UP TO 2 DAYS IN ADVANCE:** Bake cake

➡ **UP TO 2 DAYS IN ADVANCE:** Fill and mask cake and ice with buttercream

➡ **UP TO 2 DAYS IN ADVANCE:** Make fondant plaque

➡ **UP TO 1 DAY IN ADVANCE OR DAY OF EVENT:** Decorate cake with a paint-by-number design and a shell border

OPPOSITE: *An excellent birthday party activity that gets the children involved in decorating the cake by filling in the paint-by-number design with colored piping gel*

CAKE ASSEMBLY

1. Roll a large fondant plaque ¼-inch thick and cut to the dimensions of the top of the cake. Allow to dry overnight. Fill and ice the cake with buttercream. Place the fondant plaque on top of the iced cake.
2. Transfer the cake to the desired cake board or cake plate using a large offset spatula to help you ease the cake into the center of the serving dish. If you want to cover the cake board in fondant or royal icing, do so 24 hours before assembly. (See page 48–49 for cake board-covering techniques.)
3. Refrigerate the cake, covered in plastic wrap, until you are ready to decorate.

FINISHING

1. Select a simple design; it may be taken from a variety of sources, such as a coloring book, craft stamp, or greeting card. Pipe the design onto the fondant plaque with the black piping gel.
2. Number each color and write the number onto the piping bags with a marker.
3. Using the food-color markers, write the number into each area of the design that corresponds with the color that should go in that area.
4. Allow the children to fill in the design with the colored piping gel.
5. Pipe a shell border around the cake with buttercream.

Modeling

FIGURES CAN BE shaped out of a variety of décor mediums, including marzipan, modeling chocolate, pastillage, fondant, and gum paste. When designing a cake with modeled figures, keep in mind the size and height of the cake so that the figures are not overwhelming. More complex figures with multiple components can be assembled with firm royal icing once the pieces are dry, or when the pieces are still soft enough to adhere together without icing. Figures can also be small, accent pieces, such as holiday presents, pieces of fruit, or bows. If you enjoy modeling, consider investing in a clay modeling book. The techniques and materials that are used can be easily transferred to cake decorating. Fondant, gum paste, modeling chocolate, and marzipan share similarities with clay and can be worked with in a similar fashion.

To create details on models, you may choose to purchase a gum paste tool set. These sets come with several tools that are used to shape gum paste flowers, and also come in handy when making people, fruit, and many other figures. They can be purchased at craft and cake decorating stores. Keep in mind that similar tools are available in art supply stores in the clay modeling section, which may offer a greater variety of tools to choose from.

Molds used in chocolate and candy making are also great for shaping figures out of sugar paste as well. Pressing the décor medium into the molds and then allowing them to firm up in the freezer will allow the shapes to be easily released from the molds.

Modeling also includes making fondant or gum paste flowers. Flower cutters and presses are available at cake decorating stores for shaping very realistic flowers out of various décor mediums. Some flowers, such as hydrangeas and roses, do not necessarily need specific cutters or presses and can be shaped by hand. Making flowers on floral wire enables you to attach several flowers together with floral tape to create a sugar bouquet.

Gum Paste Scroll Cake Topper

Gum paste

Parchment-lined baking sheet

Cornstarch or confectioners' sugar

Royal icing (see page 41)

1. Roll a strip of gum paste into a log. Taper the log so that it is thicker in the middle and gradually becomes thinner at the ends.
2. Shape the log into a scroll and leave it to dry for 24 hours on a piece of cornstarch-dusted parchment paper.
3. Dust off any excess cornstarch.
4. Secure the scroll to the cake or to a fondant plaque with royal icing.

OPPOSITE, LEFT: *Dust the dogwood mold with cornstarch and place the dogwood cutout between the two pieces of the mold; press down lightly, remove the flower, and place it on a foam pad for shaping; use a ball tool to shape the petals of the décor medium flower by running the ball tool along the edges of the petals and applying firm pressure; shape the petals when the décor medium is soft and pliable.* CENTER: *Place the shaped petals in an egg carton or apple tray that has been dusted with cornstarch or confectioners' sugar; press décor medium through a fine sieve to create the centers of the flowers.* RIGHT: *Use a dry brush to dust a dried flower with powdered food color; do not apply too much pressure or the flower might break.*

Dogwood Flowers

1. Lightly dust the work surface with cornstarch. Roll out just enough fondant or gum paste to make small batches of flowers at a time. Cover the remaining décor medium with plastic wrap to prevent it from drying. Roll out a piece of décor medium to 1⁄16-inch thick and keep it covered with plastic wrap.

2. Use the dogwood cutter to cut out a flower. Thin the edges of the flower with a ball tool on a soft mat or piece of foam.

3. Dust the dogwood mold with cornstarch or confectioners' sugar. Place the dogwood flower in the base of the mold and place the other half on top. Press down lightly and remove the flower.

4. Use an egg carton that has been dusted with cornstarch or confectioners' sugar to shape the flower.

5. For the center, push a pea-sized piece of décor medium through the screen of a sifter. Remove the décor medium that goes through the screen with a knife and adhere it to the center of the flower with a bit of water.

6. Repeat this process with the other flowers and let them dry for 24 hours.

7. To make the flowers appear more realistic, use pale green powdered food coloring to dust around the centers of each flower. Next, accent the edges of the four petals of each flower with pink or red powdered food coloring.

Cornstarch or confectioners' sugar
Rolling pin
White fondant or gum paste
Plastic wrap
Dogwood cutters, small and medium
Dogwood silicone mold
Soft mat or a piece of foam for shaping
Ball tool
Egg carton or egg foam
Pale green and pink or red powdered food coloring

NOTE: The dogwood cutters can be exchanged for other types of flowers, such as daisies.

Gum paste, pale blue

36 pieces of thin, white floral wire

Small scissors

Floral tape

Thin knitting needle

Small pliers, for shaping the angle of the flowers in the bouquet

Anger tool (a gum paste tool with a cone at the tip) or wooden skewer

Ball tool

Gum Paste Hydrangeas

1. Create a small, thin hook at the top of each piece of floral wire with small pliers.
2. Take a small ball of gum paste and form a cone.
3. Make a hole in the fat end of the cone with the anger tool or a wooden skewer.
4. Insert the scissors into the hole and cut 4 even pieces that will form the petals.
5. Flatten the petals with your fingers.
6. Flatten and thin the petals with the large end of the ball tool.
7. Use the end of the knitting needle to make a line down the center of each petal, working from the outside to the center of each petal.
8. Insert the wire into the flower, starting with the non-hooked end.
9. Pull the wire through the flower until just the tip of the wire loop shows.
10. Allow the flowers to dry. Once dry, you can dust the flowers with powdered food coloring if desired.
11. Connect 6 flowers together by wrapping floral tape tightly around the wire "stems." Make 6 bunches of 6 flowers each.
12. Connect the 6 bunches with more floral tape. Cut off any excess wire so that the stem is not too long. You don't need more than a few inches of wire.
13. Insert the stem into the cake so the bouquet stands up.

AT RIGHT: *Use a small pair of scissors to cut a cylinder of gum paste into four triangular petals. Flatten the petals with a ball tool and indent each one with a knitting needle. Attach the flower to a thin piece of floral wire with a hooked end.*

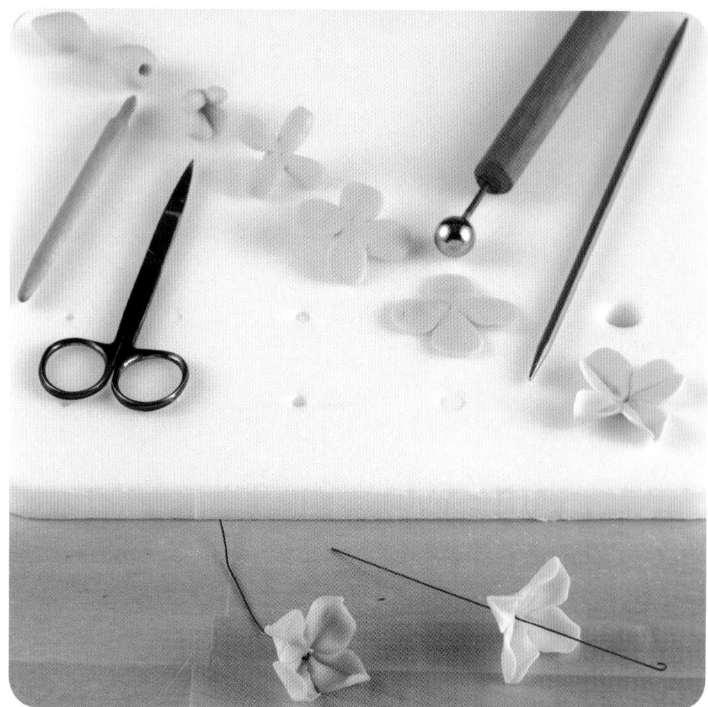

Chocolate Molds and Chocolate Sea Shells

Squeeze bottle or small spoon or small pastry brush

Tempered chocolate or coating chocolate

Silicone shell molds

Small offset spatula

Chocolate molds can be purchased in various shapes and designs from craft and cake decorating stores, as well as online cake and confections stores. Tempered chocolate and coating chocolate will set at room temperature, while untempered chocolate will need to be cooled in order to release the chocolates from the mold. One benefit of using tempered chocolate or coating chocolate is that they will not bloom (white dots that form on the chocolate) like untempered chocolate might. (See pages 44–45 for chocolate tempering techniques.)

1. Use a squeeze bottle (or a spoon or pastry brush) to line the bottoms and sides of the sea shell molds with chocolate.
2. Use a spoon or a squeeze bottle to fill the molds with chocolate. The chocolate should be flush with the sides of the mold.
3. Allow tempered chocolate or coating chocolate to set at room temperature for approximately 5 minutes before unmolding. Placing molds in the freezer for approximately 3 to 5 minutes may speed up the unmolding process.
4. Do not touch the chocolates once they are unmolded because your fingers will smudge them. Use a small offset spatula to lift the chocolates and place them on a parchment-lined baking sheet.

AT RIGHT: *Fill the silicone molds with tempered chocolate or melted coating chocolate. Tempered chocolate will set at room temperature, but the coating chocolate will need to be chilled in the freezer for approximately five minutes. Unmold the shells, taking care not to smudge the chocolate with your fingers.*

Modeling Chocolate Leaves

Modeling chocolate (see pages 36–37)

Rolling pin

Cocoa powder or confectioners' sugar

Plastic wrap

Leaf cutters

Leaf veiner, if available

1. Knead a small amount of modeling chocolate until it is pliable.
2. Lightly dust the work surface with cocoa powder (for dark modeling chocolate) or confectioners' sugar (for white modeling chocolate). Roll out a piece of modeling chocolate until it is 1⁄16-inch thick.
3. Cut out the leaves with the leaf cutter. Gather the excess modeling chocolate and wrap it tightly in plastic wrap so it does not dry out. Cover the leaf cutouts with a piece of plastic wrap.
4. Dust the leaf veiner with additional cocoa powder or confectioners' sugar.
5. Vein each leaf and store on a parchment-lined baking sheet. Leaves can be folded on the center line slightly and the tip bent back to make them look more lifelike.

1 recipe modeling chocolate (see pages 36–37)

Rolling pin

Cocoa powder or confectioners' sugar

1¼-inch round cutter

1½-inch round cutter (optional)

Plastic wrap

Plastic hand scraper

NOTE: These same techniques can be applied to making roses out of marzipan and gum paste as well. For each new row of petals to be added to a rose, make sure to use an uneven number of petals, such as 5 petals followed by 7 petals, etc. This will give the rose a more realistic appearance.

Modeling Chocolate Roses

1. Knead the modeling chocolate until it is pliable.
2. Create the center of the rose by shaping a ball of modeling chocolate that is 1 inch in diameter into a cone 1½ inches long, then roll the tip of the cone on the work surface so that it is thin. Flatten the bottom of the center so that it stands up on its own.
3. Lightly dust the work surface with cocoa powder (for dark modeling chocolate) or confectioners' sugar (for white modeling chocolate). Roll out a piece of modeling chocolate until it is 1⁄16 inch thick.
4. Cut out 5 circles with a 1¼-inch cutter to use as petals. Remove the excess modeling chocolate and wrap it tightly in plastic wrap. Cover the circles with plastic wrap when not working with them.
5. Dust the work surface with additional cocoa powder or confectioners' sugar. Place the first circle on the work surface and gently flatten the edges of the circle with the plastic scraper so that the petal edges will be thin and delicate. Repeat with each of the remaining circles.
6. Two petals will be used to make the bud. Place the cone in the center of the first petal (approximately ½ inch of the petal should be above the tip of the cone). Wrap the right side of the petal around the cone, then the left over the right. Smooth the

base of the petal into the center of the rose. Repeat this process with the other petal. For a more realistic appearance, tuck the petal inside the previous one so that they overlap slightly.

7. The next row needs three slightly overlapping petals that are attached to the bud. Curl back the edge of one side of each petal and attach the petals so the uncurled side is tucked into the previous petal.

8. To make a larger rose, repeat this process with an additional row of five petals that have been cut out with a 1½-inch round cutter.

OPPOSITE, LEFT: Shape a cone center with a thin tip; roll out the modeling chocolate to 1⁄16 inch and cut out five 1¼-inch circles; keep them covered with plastic wrap; to form the petals, use a plastic hand scraper to flatten the edge of each of the cut circles and again cover with plastic wrap. OPPOSITE RIGHT: To make the bud, attach the two petals to the base so that they overlap slightly; attach the first petal by connecting it to the tip of the base and wrapping it around. BELOW LEFT: Curl back the edge of one side of each of the three petals. CENTER: Attach the petals to the base so the uncurled side is tucked into the previous petal; a bit of water will help to secure the petals in place. RIGHT: Each additional layer needs an uneven number of petals, so the next layer has five petals, the layer after that seven, and so on.

Modeled Figures

Fondant, gum paste, or marzipan come to life with these sensational farm animals and fantasy creatures.

Chicken

(LEFT) To make the chicken, form a large ball and two smaller balls out of yellow paste. Shape the larger ball into a sausage that is tapered at both ends. Pull up one end and shape a triangle for the tail. Elongate the other end to make the neck and create a ball at the tip of the neck for a head. Pull the neck up so that the head is upright. Make an orange beak and small red triangles for under the beak and the top of the head. Taper the two smaller balls at one end and flatten the pieces. Attach the wings to the birds with the wider end facing upwards.

Horse

(PAGE 100, FIRST COLUMN) Form a round ball of brown paste and taper it at one end for the body. Shape the legs out of small balls of brown paste and attach the black hooves. Roll out cylindrical strips of light brown fondant for the tail. Shape the head by making a cylinder and flattening one end where the mouth will be. Cut a slit in the mouth area and insert a strip of white paste for the teeth. Make indents for the nostrils and attach the ears and eyes with a little bit of water or royal icing.

__OPPOSITE:__ Any creature, whether real or magical, can be shaped out of sugar paste. Once you have made one type of figure, you will discover that many others can be made using the same techniques. For example, the unicorn, puppy, and bunny are made using the same techniques as the pig and the cow (see page 100–101) with only slight color and detail variations.

Cow

(OPPOSITE, SECOND COLUMN) Form a large ball of white paste for the body and a slightly smaller one for the head. Use small amounts of black paste to create the spots. Attach small pieces of black paste to smaller balls of white paste and shape the balls into cylindrical arms and legs. Taper the arms and legs slightly at the end that will be attached to the body. Roll a thin, red strip for the collar and make a bell out of yellow paste. Create the nose by elongating a round cutout and making two indentations for the nostrils. Attach the ears, eyes, and nose with a little bit of water or royal icing.

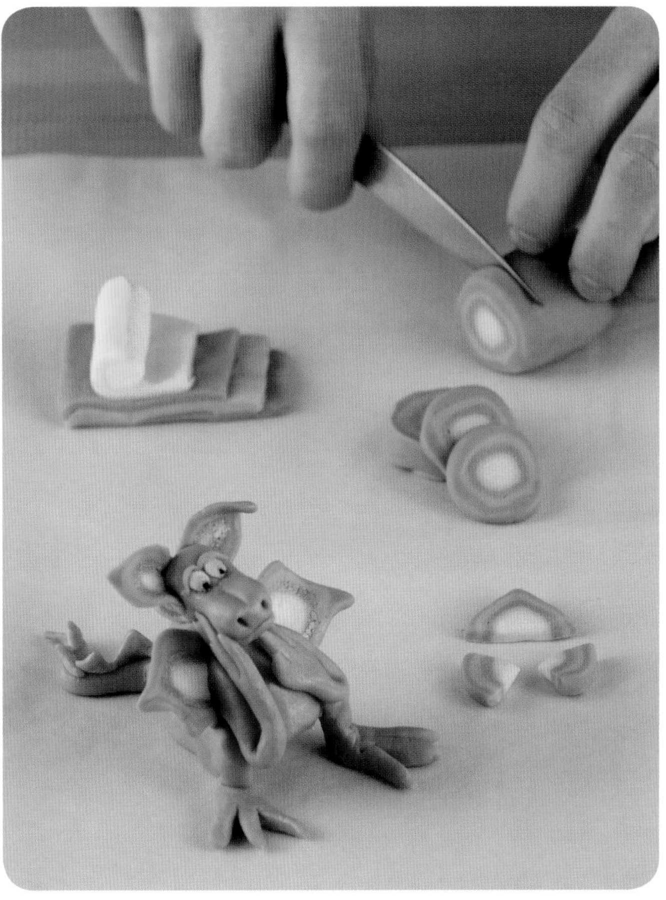

Pig

(OPPOSITE, THIRD COLUMN) Form a large ball of pink paste for the body and a slightly smaller one for the head. Shape four smaller balls into cylindrical arms and legs. Taper the arms and legs slightly at the end that will be attached to the body. Taper a cylinder of pink paste and curl the end to create the tail. Create the nose by elongating a round cutout and making two indentations for the nostrils. Attach the ears, eyes, and nose with a little bit of water or royal icing.

Sheep

(OPPOSITE, FOURTH COLUMN) Form a large cone of white paste for the body. Form a smaller cone of brown paste for the head and attach it to the body. Flatten two cones of brown paste for the ears. Shape four small balls of brown paste into cylinders for the arms and legs and attach black paste at one end of each piece for the hooves. Form tiny white balls of paste and attach them to the body to create the wool. Indent a mouth and nose on the head and attach the eyes and ears with a little bit of water or royal icing. Attach a few round balls of white paste to the top of the sheep's head.

ABOVE RIGHT: *To create the multi-toned sugar paste for the dragon, roll a tube of colored sugar paste. Roll out rectangles of other colored sugar paste to the width of the tube and wrap the tube in each layer. Roll it slightly to close the seam. Cut pieces width-wise out of the larger tube and either shape figures or roll it flat for making cutouts.*

Boy on a Toy Truck

(OPPOSITE) For the boy, begin by shaping two large balls of paste for the body and head, medium-size balls for the arms and legs, and smaller ones for the hands, shoes, and hat. (See photo at left for the colors.) Roll a ball of paste into a strip and cut out pieces for the hair. Attach the pieces to the head with water. Roll the arms and legs into logs that are tapered at one end. Flatten the other end and attach shoes to the legs and hands to the arms. Shape the hat, nose, and eyes and attach them to the head. For the truck, shape two large balls out of green paste and make two more balls that are slightly smaller. Shape one of the larger balls into the base of the truck and shape the other ball into the seat by flattening it into a rectangle. Shape the two smaller balls into the front of the truck. Make the headlights out of small circles of green and white paste and attach them to the front of the truck. Make the wheels by flattening four small balls of green paste and inserting tiny black balls of paste into the center of each. Attach the boy's legs to the truck and then attach the back wheels. Assemble the rest of the boy on the truck. Attach the front end and the front wheels to the truck. You may need a small amount of water or royal icing to attach the different parts securely.

Marzipan Fruit

Marzipan

Paste or powdered food colors: green, yellow, brown, orange, red, and purple

Cloves, for apple stems

Clean, food-safe paint brush

Nutmeg grater, for texturing fruit

VARIATION:

If you do not have marzipan, fondant or gum paste can be colored and used to make fruit.

1. To make an apple, knead a small amount of food coloring into the marzipan until it is pale green. Shape a ½-ounce piece of the green marzipan into a ball. Break a clove into two parts. The long part is inserted into the top of the apple as the stem and the star-shaped part is inserted into the bottom of the apple. Paint the fruit with pale red and green food colors or dust with powdered food colors.

2. To make a banana, color the marzipan yellow. Shape a small piece of marzipan into a curved tube with flat ends. Paint areas of the banana, especially the tips, with brown food color.

3. To make lemons and oranges, color the marzipan either yellow or orange. Give lemons a slightly oblong shape, whereas oranges should be round. Gently roll the fruit over a nutmeg grater or another fine grater to give them a realistic texture.

4. To make pumpkins, color the marzipan bright orange. Shape a ½-ounce piece of marzipan into a ball. Using the blunt side of a paring knife, create indents in the sides of the pumpkin. Insert a small, green stem made of marzipan.

5. To make blackberries or raspberries, color the marzipan either dark purple or red. Roll tiny balls of marzipan and gently press the balls together forming a slightly oblong shape. Either insert green stems into the berries or gently flatten the tops of the berries.

Marshmallow Flowers and Designs for Cupcakes

Large marshmallows

Scissors

Sanding sugar or colored nonpareils

Powdered food color

Gumdrops

The same technique can be applied to mini-marshmallows or colored marshmallows.

1. Color the sanding sugar or the nonpareils by mixing them in a bowl with a small amount of powdered food coloring. Adjust the amount of food coloring to achieve the desired shade. If you make the sanding sugar too dark in color, simply add more plain sugar to the bowl and combine with the colored sugar.

2. Cut marshmallows into quarters width-wise with scissors or a knife.

3. Dip the sticky ends of the marshmallows in colored sanding sugar or the nonpareils.

4. Arrange the colored marshmallows into flowers or other designs on top of cakes or cupcakes.

5. Use gumdrops or other candy for the centers of the flowers.

Projects

SERVES 10 TO 12

Blush Pink Hearts and Roses Cake

PREPARATION TIMELINE

- **UP TO 2 WEEKS IN ADVANCE:** (minimum of 24 hours) Prepare and assemble heart box
- **UP TO 1 WEEK IN ADVANCE:** Prepare modeling chocolate
- **UP TO 3 DAYS IN ADVANCE:** Prepare modeling chocolate roses and leaves
- **UP TO 2 DAYS IN ADVANCE:** Cover cake board in fondant, if needed
- **UP TO 2 DAYS IN ADVANCE:** Bake cake
- **UP TO 1 DAY IN ADVANCE:** Cover cake in fondant; make fondant band
- **DAY OF EVENT:** Finish decorating cake

OPPOSITE: *A heart-shaped cake with a fondant décor band, pastillage gift box, and modeling chocolate roses*

Components

One 9-inch heart-shaped cake, filled and masked in buttercream

1 white pastillage heart-shaped box (see Gum Paste or Pastillage Heart Box, page 130, for method)

4–5 white modeling chocolate roses in shades of pink (see Modeling Chocolate Roses, page 96, for method)

5–6 white modeling chocolate leaves (see Modeling Chocolate Leaves, page 95, for method)

Fondant décor band (see Fondant Décor Band, pages 124–125, for method)

Equipment and Materials

CAKE ASSEMBLY

1¾ pounds fondant, shaded blush pink with gel food coloring

Cornstarch

Rolling pin

Fondant smoothers

Knife

Small pin

Large offset palette knife

PASTILLAGE HEART BOX

Cornstarch

Rolling pin

Pastillage (see page 39)

Pizza wheel or knife

Parchment-lined baking sheet

Set of heart-shaped cutters

Pastry bag fitted with a #1 tip

White royal icing

Food color pen or colored royal icing for inscription

MODELING CHOCOLATE ROSES AND LEAVES

1 recipe white modeling chocolate (see page 37)

Oil-based food coloring

Rolling pin

1¼-inch round cutter

Plastic wrap

Confectioners' sugar

Plastic hand scraper

Leaf cutter

Leaf veiner (optional)

FONDANT DÉCOR BAND

Plastic, flexible tape measure

Cornstarch

8 ounces white fondant

Rolling pin

Plastic wrap

Small heart-shaped cutters, 2–3 sizes

4 ounces fondant in shades of pink, blue, and green

Small circle cutters or piping tips of various sizes

Pizza wheel or sharp knife

Cup of water

Pastry brush

Happy Anniversary

VARIATIONS:

The roses and leaves can be made out of marzipan or gum paste instead of modeling chocolate. Other blush shades, such as purple, yellow, or blue, could be substituted, and are perfect for a bridal or baby shower cake. Many other shaped cutters could be used to make the fondant décor band. Small blossom plunger cutters would be ideal for making a floral print band.

CAKE ASSEMBLY

1. Roll the blush pink fondant into a circle ⅜-inch thick and approximately 15 inches in diameter. The fondant circle needs to be large enough to completely enrobe the cake. Dust the fondant lightly with cornstarch and roll the piece of fondant around a rolling pin. Drape the fondant over the cake and smooth the edges with the palms of your hands or with a fondant smoother. Trim the fondant around the edge of the cake with a knife or pizza wheel and remove any bubbles that form in the fondant with a small pin (see pages 53–55 for cake covering techniques).

2. Transfer the cake to the desired cake board or cake plate using a large offset palette knife to help you ease the cake into the center of the serving dish. If you want to cover the cake board in fondant or royal icing, do so 24 hours before assembly (see pages 48–49 for cake board-covering techniques).

FINISHING

1. Use a food color pen or colored royal icing for the inscription. If using royal icing, fill a pastry bag or paper cornet halfway with colored royal icing and secure the ends. Write or pipe a message on the lid to the pastillage box, embellishing it in any way you like. You can pipe hearts and vines with the plain tip or switch the tips to pipe leaves, flowers, and stars.

2. Secure the base of the pastillage box to the top of the cake with a little royal icing. Determine how you want the lid to rest on the side of the box. You can secure the lid to the box with royal icing or rest it against the box. Gently arrange the roses and leaves inside the box and around it. Be careful not to crack the fragile pastillage lid. Roses and leaves that will be outside the box should be secured to the cake with a small amount of royal icing.

Chocolate Rose and Butterfly Cake

Components

One 10-inch cake, filled and masked in buttercream (see pages 50–51 for information on filling and stacking tiered cakes)

One 8-inch cake, filled and masked in buttercream

One 6-inch cake, filled and masked in buttercream

3 large white modeling chocolate roses, in shades of peach (see Modeling Chocolate Roses, page 96, for method)

10 white modeling chocolate buds, in shades of peach (see Modeling Chocolate Roses, page 96, for method)

10 white modeling chocolate leaves (see Modeling Chocolate Leaves, page 95, for method)

Chocolate butterflies (see Piping Chocolate Décor, page 69, for method)

Fondant bands for each tier (see Fondant Décor Bands, page 124, for method)

Equipment and Materials

CAKE ASSEMBLY

4½ pounds peach fondant

16 straws for dowels

Cornstarch

Rolling pin

Fondant smoothers

Knife

Small pin

Large offset palette knife

Scissors for cutting straw dowels

Royal icing

MODELING CHOCOLATE ROSES, BUDS, AND LEAVES

1 recipe white modeling chocolate (see page 37)

Oil-based food coloring

Rolling pin

1¼-inch round cutter

1½-inch round cutter

1¾-inch round cutter

Plastic wrap

Confectioners' sugar

Plastic hand scraper

Leaf cutters

Leaf veiner, if available

CHOCOLATE BUTTERFLIES

Acetate sheet, or page protectors, or parchment paper

Paper cornets or a piping bag with #1 tip

Tempered chocolate or coating chocolate

Butterfly pattern (see Templates, page 196)

FONDANT BANDS

Plastic, flexible tape measure

Cornstarch

1 pound pale green fondant

Rolling pin

Plastic wrap

Pizza wheel or sharp knife

Cup of water

Pastry brush

PREPARATION TIMELINE

➡ **UP TO 1 WEEK IN ADVANCE:** Prepare modeling chocolate

➡ **UP TO 1 WEEK IN ADVANCE:** Prepare modeling chocolate roses, leaves, and buds

➡ **UP TO 2 DAYS IN ADVANCE:** Prepare chocolate butterflies

➡ **UP TO 2 DAYS IN ADVANCE:** Cover cake board in fondant

➡ **UP TO 2 DAYS IN ADVANCE:** Bake cake

➡ **UP TO 2 DAYS IN ADVANCE:** Fill and mask cake and cover cake with fondant

➡ **UP TO 2 DAYS IN ADVANCE:** Assemble cake

➡ **UP TO 1 DAY IN ADVANCE OR DAY OF EVENT:** Decorate cake

CAKE ASSEMBLY

1. Begin by covering the 10-inch cake. Roll 2 pounds of fondant into a circle ⅜-inch thick and large enough to completely enrobe the cake. Dust the fondant lightly with cornstarch and roll the piece of fondant around a rolling pin. Drape the fondant over the cake and smooth the edges with the palms of your hands or with the fondant smoothers. Trim the fondant around the edge of the cake and remove any bubbles that form in the fondant with a small pin (see pages 53–55 for cake covering techniques).

2. Repeat with the remaining two cakes, using 1½ pounds of fondant for the 8-inch cake and 1 pound of fondant for the 6-inch cake.

3. Transfer the largest cake to the desired cake board or cake plate using a large offset spatula to help you ease the cake into the center of the serving dish. If you want to cover the cake board in fondant or royal icing, do so 24 hours before assembly (see pages 48–49 for cake board-covering techniques).

4. Insert one of the straws into the center of the cake and mark where the straw is flush with the cake. Cut 8 additional straws to the same height as the first. Insert 6 of the straws into the cake in a circle and place the remaining 3 straws in the center of the cake. Use an 8-inch cake pan to help you guide the placement of the straws (see page 57 for doweling techniques).

5. Dab a small amount of royal icing or buttercream on top of each support. Using a large offset palette knife, place the 8-inch cake on top of the base cake, making sure it is perfectly centered and level. Insert another straw into the center of this cake and mark where the straw is flush with the cake. Cut the remaining straws to this height. Insert 5 straws into the cake in a circle and place 2 in the middle of the cake. Use a 6-inch cake pan to help you guide the placement of the straws.

6. Dab icing on each of the dowels and place the 6-inch cake on top of the middle cake. Press the cake down gently so that it is secure.

7. Refrigerate the cake, covered in plastic wrap, until you are ready to decorate.

FINISHING

1. Make the pale green bands and place them around the base of each tier (see Fondant Décor Bands, page 124).

2. Arrange the 3 large roses, 3 buds, and 6 to 7 leaves on the top of the cake. Secure them in place with royal icing.

3. On each tier, secure 2 to 3 buds and 2 leaves to the cake.

4. Secure the chocolate butterflies to the cake with the tempered chocolate or melted coating chocolate.

VARIATIONS

The cake could be decorated with dark, milk, or white chocolate roses or a combination of all three. Similarly, the butterflies can be made out of dark, milk, or white tempered chocolate. Dragonflies, flowers, and other decorations can be piped with tempered chocolate to enhance the cake's appearance.

OPPOSITE: *A beautiful multi-tiered cake with peach modeling chocolate roses, modeling chocolate leaves, and piped chocolate butterflies*

SERVES 18 TO 22

Dogwood Cake

PREPARATION TIMELINE

- UP TO 2 WEEKS IN ADVANCE: Prepare gum paste dogwoods
- UP TO 2 WEEKS IN ADVANCE: Prepare gum paste scroll
- UP TO 1 WEEK IN ADVANCE: Prepare fondant plaques
- UP TO 2 DAYS IN ADVANCE: Cover cake board in fondant
- UP TO 2 DAYS IN ADVANCE: Bake cake
- UP TO 2 DAYS IN ADVANCE: Fill and mask cake and cover cake with fondant
- UP TO 2 DAYS IN ADVANCE: Assemble cake
- UP TO 1 DAY IN ADVANCE OR DAY OF EVENT: Decorate cake

OPPOSITE: *Blush pink dogwoods, white vines, a personalized fondant plaque, and a gum paste scroll cake topper*

Components

One 8-inch round cake, filled and masked in buttercream (see pages 50–51 for information on filling and stacking tiered cakes)

One 6-inch round cake, filled and masked in buttercream

White fondant or gum paste dogwoods (see Dogwood Flowers, page 93, for method)

Round fondant plaque, blush pink (see Fondant Plaques, page 127, for method)

Gum paste scroll (see Gum Paste Scroll Cake Topper, page 92, for method)

White oval plaque for inscription (see Fondant Plaques, page 127, for method)

Blush pink fondant décor bands (see Fondant Décor Band, page 124, for method)

Equipment and Materials

CAKE ASSEMBLY

2½ pounds blush pink fondant

7 straws for dowels

Cornstarch

Rolling pin

Fondant smoothers

Knife

Small pin

Large offset palette knife

Scissors for cutting straw dowels

FONDANT OR GUM PASTE DOGWOODS

Rolling pin

8 ounces white fondant or gum paste

Cornstarch or confectioners' sugar

Plastic wrap

Dogwood cutters, small and medium

Dogwood silicone mold

Soft mat or a piece of foam for shaping

Ball tool

Apple tray or egg carton

Pale green and pink or red powdered food coloring

GUM PASTE SCROLL CAKE TOPPER

Gum paste

Parchment-lined baking sheet

Royal icing

FONDANT PLAQUES

8 ounces white fondant

Rolling pin

Cornstarch

Circle and oval cutters

Parchment-lined baking sheet

Small offset palette knife

Food color marker for the inscription

FONDANT BANDS

Plastic, flexible tape measure

Cornstarch

1 pound white fondant

Rolling pin

Plastic wrap

Pizza wheel or sharp knife

Cup of water

Pastry brush

It's a Girl

VARIATIONS:

There are many other larger flower cutters available, such as daisies that can replace the dogwoods as the theme of the cake.

CAKE ASSEMBLY

1. Begin by covering the 8-inch cake. Roll out 1½ pounds of pink fondant into a circle ⅜-inch thick that is large enough to completely enrobe the cake. Dust the fondant lightly with cornstarch and roll the piece of fondant around a rolling pin. Drape the fondant over the cake and smooth the edges with the palms of your hands or with the fondant smoothers. Trim the fondant around the edge of the cake and remove any bubbles that form in the fondant with a small pin (see pages 53–55 for cake covering techniques). Repeat with the 6-inch cake, using 1 pound of fondant.

2. Transfer the 8-inch cake to the desired cake board or cake plate using a large offset spatula to help you ease the cake into the center of the serving dish. If you want to cover the cake board in fondant or royal icing, do so 24 hours before assembly (see pages 48–49 for cake board-covering techniques).

3. Insert one of the straws into the center of the cake and mark where the straw is flush with the top of the cake. Cut all of the straws to this height. Insert 5 straws into the cake in a circle and place 2 in the middle of the cake. Use a 6-inch cake pan to help you guide the placement of the straws.

4. Dab a small amount of royal icing on top of each dowel. Using a large offset palette knife, place the 6-inch cake on top of the base cake, making sure it is perfectly centered and level. Press the cake down gently so that it is secure (see page 57 for multi-tiered cake assembly techniques).

5. Refrigerate the cake, covered in plastic wrap, until you are ready to decorate.

FINISHING

1. Make the fondant bands and place them around the base of each tier (see Fondant Décor Bands, page 124).

2. Roll out thin logs of white fondant and attach them to the cake with royal icing. These will be the vines.

3. Using a piping bag of white royal icing fitted with a #1 tip, attach the dogwoods to the cake, evenly spacing them out.

4. Secure the gum paste scroll to the circular plaque with royal icing. Secure the plaque to the cake with more icing and attach two or three small dogwood flowers to the scroll.

5. Write an inscription onto the oval plaque and attach it to the cake with royal icing. It can either lay flat on the cake or rest against the scroll.

SERVES 12 TO 14

Wizard Cake

Components

One 9-inch square cake filled and iced with buttercream

Fondant dragon (see page 101 for method)

Fondant wizard (see page 99 for method)

Shooting star plaque (see Fondant Shooting Star Plaque, page 127 for method)

Blue fondant band (see Fondant Décor Band, page 124 for method)

Equipment and Materials

CAKE ASSEMBLY

2 pounds yellow fondant

Fondant smoothers

Knife

Rolling pin

Cornstarch

Large offset palette knife

FONDANT CUTOUTS

4 ounces each blue, green, and purple fondant

Star, triangle, and spiral cutters

SHOOTING STAR PLAQUE

4 ounces blue fondant

Cornstarch

Rolling pin

Shooting star template (page 198)

Knife

Food color marker

FONDANT BAND

Plastic, flexible tape measure

8 ounces blue fondant

Rolling pin

Pizza wheel or knife

Cornstarch

PREPARATION TIMELINE

➡ **UP TO 2 WEEKS IN ADVANCE:**
Prepare fondant dragon and wizard

➡ **UP TO 1 WEEK IN ADVANCE:**
Prepare the shooting star plaque

➡ **UP TO 2 DAYS IN ADVANCE:**
Cover cake board in fondant if not using a cake plate

➡ **UP TO 2 DAYS IN ADVANCE:**
Bake cake

➡ **UP TO 2 DAYS IN ADVANCE:**
Fill and mask cake and cover cake with fondant

➡ **DAY OF EVENT:**
Decorate cake

Happy Birthday Spencer

CAKE ASSEMBLY

1. Begin by covering the cake with fondant. Roll out the yellow fondant into a ⅛- to ¼-inch-thick square that is large enough to completely enrobe the cake. Dust the fondant lightly with cornstarch and roll the piece of fondant around a rolling pin. Drape the fondant over the cake and smooth the edges with the palms of your hands or fondant smoothers. Trim the fondant around the edge of the cake and remove any bubbles that form in the fondant with a small pin. (See pages 53–55 for cake covering techniques.)
2. Transfer the cake to the desired cake board or cake plate using a large offset spatula to help you ease the cake into the center of the serving dish. If you want to cover the cake board in fondant or royal icing, do so 24 hours before assembly. (See pages 48–49 for cake board-covering techniques.)
3. Refrigerate the cake, covered in plastic wrap, until you are ready to decorate.

FINISHING

1. Make the fondant band and attach it to the base of the cake with a little water.
2. Roll out the green, blue, and purple fondant and make the triangle, star, and spiral cutouts. Attach the cutouts to the cake with a bit of water.
3. Place the dragon and the wizard on the cake or on the serving dish. If desired, attach the figures to the cake with royal icing.
4. Use two pearls of the blue fondant to prop the plaque up on the cake.

OPPOSITE: *A golden cake decorated with fondant stars, dots, and spirals and fondant or gum paste figurines. The wizard was shaped freehand and is a great example of using your imagination to take a cake to new heights.*

MAKES 24 CUPCAKES

Farm Animal Cupcakes

PREPARATION TIMELINE

- **UP TO 1 WEEK IN ADVANCE:** Prepare the modeled animals
- **UP TO 2 DAYS IN ADVANCE:** Make the cupcakes
- **DAY OF EVENT:** Decorate the cupcakes

Components

Cupcakes

Farm animal figures (see pages 98–101)

Equipment and Materials

Buttercream or ganache for icing

Fondant, gum paste, or marzipan

Food color

Small offset spatula

Brown and green jimmies

Red check ribbon

FINISHING

1. Ice the cupcakes with buttercream or ganache. The icing can be piped onto the cupcakes into a design or it can be spread over the cupcakes with a small palette knife.
2. Pour the brown and green jimmies into separate bowls. Dip the cupcakes into the jimmies so that they cover the icing.
3. Tie a bow around each cupcake with the red check ribbon.
4. Make the animal figures and place them on top of the cupcakes.

OPPOSITE: *Adorable farm animal cupcakes decorated with fondant figures, red check ribbon, and brown and green jimmies*

Chapter Eight

Stencils and Cutouts

STENCILS AND CUTOUTS are easy to make and can be embellished in numerous ways. Personalized messages can be piped onto fondant or chocolate plaques; special themes or holidays can be expressed by using shaped cookie cutters; and there is no limit to the number of designs that can be painted or piped onto a cake using stencils, which can be purchased inexpensively at craft stores. In addition, stencils can be made by cutting shapes out of parchment paper or cardboard. Outline the design onto the paper or cardboard with a pencil and then cut it out with scissors or an X-acto knife.

Stencils and cutouts can involve a wide variety of décor mediums. Plaques and cutouts can be made of fondant, pastillage, gum paste, and modeling chocolate. Three-dimensional figures and structures, such as gift boxes, can be made by cutting out pastillage, fondant, or gum paste pieces. Royal icing and meringue can be spread over a stencil and then allowed to dry. These décor pieces can then be embellished with many techniques, including piping and dusting with powdered food color or luster dusts.

Chocolate cutouts are both delicious and striking garnishes for a cake. Tempered chocolate makes very shiny and crisp décor pieces. Coating chocolate, which is available at craft and candy stores, also works well and comes in a variety of colors. To create

a colorful pattern on chocolate cutouts, purchase oil-based food colors and spread them in a design on top of the acetate or page protector that is used to make the cutouts. Another option is to color white chocolate and pipe a design onto the acetate before spreading the final layer of chocolate. The pattern of the food colors or the white chocolate will transpose onto the chocolate as it sets. Shaping the pieces will add yet another dimension to chocolate cutouts. Simply cut the acetate into the desired shape and, after spreading the chocolate onto the acetate, place it in a mold until it sets. The mold can be as simple as a cup or a paper towel roll that has been cut in half. Carefully peel away the acetate to reveal an elegantly curved chocolate garnish.

Stencils and Tamping

Tamping brushes are short brushes or sticks with a soft, foam-covered blunt end. They can be purchased at craft stores and are ideal for imprinting a stencil design into soft décor medium. You can stencil onto plaques or directly onto a cake itself. Place the stencil on top of the soft décor medium and press the tamping brush into the medium using the stencil as a guide. Remove the stencil and the image will be imprinted into the décor medium. Allow the décor to dry completely before using.

BELOW LEFT: *A gallery of assorted decorative cutouts. Sets of shapes or individual cookie cutters can be purchased to make plaques and designs, such as the stars, the pumpkins, and the butterfly. Other designs can be cut out of the décor medium by using a stencil or a template, such as the castle walls and the fence posts.*

BELOW RIGHT: *Place the stencil on top of the soft décor medium and, using the stencil as a guide, apply color with the tamping brush to the décor medium; remove the stencil and the image will be imprinted on the décor medium. This versatile technique can be done with any stencil and any type of décor medium. It is used to create the reindeer on the plaques for the Holiday Cupcakes shown on page 191.*

Royal Icing Butterflies

Butterfly wing stencil (see Templates, page 196)

White royal icing

Small offset palette knife

White flower stamens (see Shopping Resources, page 195)

Acrylic or metal bars

1. Place the wing stencil on a parchment-lined baking sheet.
2. Spread royal icing evenly over the stencil with the offset palette knife. Be sure to make the wings the same thickness as the plastic stencil, not thicker. You will need two wings for each butterfly.
3. Allow the royal icing to dry until firm. It will dry at room temperature.
4. To assemble the butterflies, carefully remove each of the wings from the parchment paper.
5. Pipe a line of tiny dots with royal icing on a piece of parchment paper that will be the butterfly's body. Insert two stamens at the top of the piped body for the antennae.
6. Place the bars on either side of the body and insert the wings into the body at an angle while the royal icing is still wet. The wings should rest against the bars. Allow the butterfly to dry for several hours before handling.

BELOW, LEFT: *Spread royal icing evenly over the butterfly wing stencil with an offset palette knife; make the wings either on a piece of parchment paper or on a baking mat.* **CENTER:** *Pipe evenly spaced lines of connected dots out of royal icing; these will be the butterflies' bodies.* **RIGHT:** *Insert the butterfly wings into the bodies at an angle and allow them to dry as they lean against the metal or acrylic bars; once they are dry they can be removed and attached to the cake.*

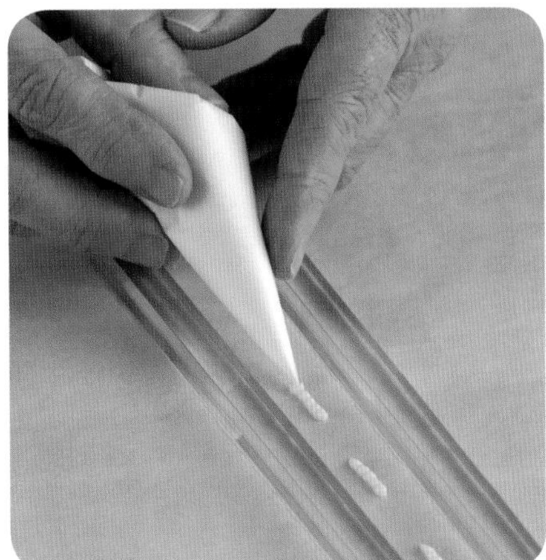

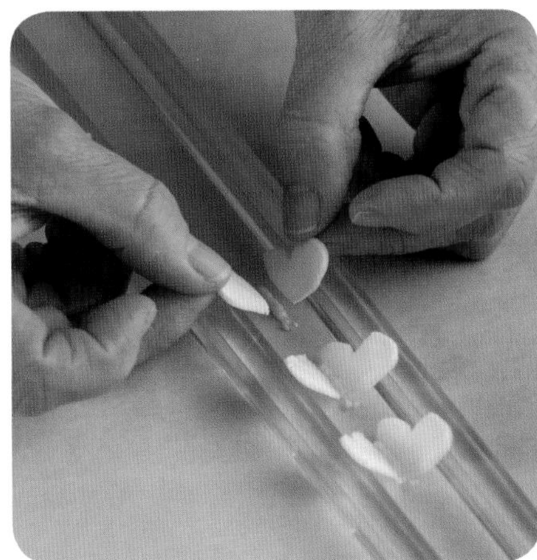

Fondant, Gum Paste, and Pastillage Décor

Fondant Décor Band

- Flexible tape measure
- White fondant for band
- Cornstarch
- Rolling pin
- Plastic wrap
- Small heart-shape cutters, 2–3 different sizes
- Fondant in various colors for cutouts
- Small circle cutters or piping tips of various sizes
- Ruler
- Pizza cutter
- Pastry brush
- Cup of water
- Paring knife

As used on the Blush Pink Hearts and Roses Cake on page 106.

1. Measure the base perimeter of the cake with a flexible, plastic tape measure. The band will need to be 2 inches longer than the perimeter of the cake to fit around the cake properly.
2. Dust the work surface with cornstarch and roll out the white fondant into a strip about two-thirds the length you need for the band, and a minimum of 1½ inches wide. Cover the fondant thoroughly in plastic wrap.
3. On a surface lightly dusted with cornstarch, roll out the three different shades of pink fondant one at a time to ⅛ inch in thickness. Cut out hearts and circles of various sizes with the cutters and cover the shapes with plastic wrap to prevent them from drying.
4. Place the cutouts in a random pattern on top of the white fondant strip and press down gently. When not applying the cutouts, make sure the fondant is well covered.
5. Dust the rolling pin lightly with cornstarch. Roll the fondant strip out to the needed length.
6. Measure the strip of fondant to make sure it is long enough. Using a long ruler and the pizza cutter, trim the strip of fondant so that it has a smooth edge running lengthwise. The band should be 1 inch wide. Cut the strip with a pizza cutter.
7. Remove the excess pieces of fondant. Dust any excess cornstarch off of the band with a pastry brush. Gently roll up the fondant band so it is in a small coil. This will allow you to unroll the band onto the cake.

8. With a pastry brush, apply a small amount of water around the base of the cake where the fondant band will go. Try not to get water on the rest of the cake because it will leave a shiny spot.

9. Begin unrolling the band starting at the top part of the heart where the crease is. As you unroll the band, make sure that it sits flat on the base with no gap at the bottom of the cake.

10. Continue to unroll the band around the cake. You may need to re-dampen the base of the cake so that the band will adhere securely to it.

11. To make a perfect seam, overlap the two ends of the band and with a sharp paring knife, cut the band so that the two ends will perfectly meet in a straight line at the crevice of the heart.

AT RIGHT: *Measure the circumference of the cake to determine the length of the band; roll fondant into a log; make fondant cutouts that will go onto the band (stars and dots are shown here); roll out the log into a band and place the decorative pieces on top; roll the designs flat onto the band; use a ruler or a template to cut out the band to the desired thickness with a pizza wheel; roll up the band into a small spiral.*

- Cornstarch pouch for dusting (see page 38)
- Rolling pin
- Gum paste or fondant
- Ruler
- Pizza wheel or sharp knife
- Water
- Parchment-lined baking sheet
- White floral wire (one piece for each loop and end)
- White floral tape

VARIATIONS:

Changing the width and length of the ribbons so that they are thinner will give your bow a more delicate appearance.

Gum Paste or Fondant Bows and Ribbons

To make the two-toned ribbon for the Gift Wrapped Cake on page 142, use the following technique, but roll out two different colors of fondant or gum paste. Brush off all the cornstarch or confectioners' sugar from each color and fuse the two colors together by placing one on top of the other. Dust the surface with more cornstarch and roll the décor medium until it is ⅛-inch thick. If desired, run a crimping wheel along the sides of each ribbon or loop before the décor medium dries. (Use the crimping wheel on the loop before you fold it over.)

1. Dust the work surface with cornstarch or confectioners' sugar. Roll out a piece of fondant or gum paste until it is ⅛-inch thick.
2. Cut the décor medium into a rectangle using the pizza cutter. Cut equal size strips out of the larger rectangle with the pizza cutter. Cut the strips as thick or as thin as you want the bows to be.
3. To make the loops, taper each end of the strip into a point using a paring knife. Dab a small amount of water at each end of the strip. Place a piece of floral wire at the base of one end of the strip. Fold the strip in half, using your fingers to create a large loop. Press down gently to secure the two ends together.
4. Turn the loop on its side and allow it to dry on a flat piece of parchment paper. Allow the loops to dry for a minimum of 24 hours.
5. Make 12 to 15 loops for a large bow and 6 to 8 for a smaller bow.
6. To make the ribbon ends, use fondant strips the same size as the ones used to make the loops. Using a paring knife, cut a V-shaped notch from one end of each strip, and taper the other end into a point.
7. Dab a small amount of water at the end of the ribbon and place a piece of floral wire on top. Wrap the moist décor medium around the wire and pinch to secure.
8. Use an egg carton to shape the ribbon and let it dry for 24 hours. Repeat this process to make as many ribbons as you would like.
9. Once the components are dry, use floral tape to tie the loops and the ribbons together. Do not shape any of the pieces by pulling on the décor medium because they might break. Adjust the wire and this will automatically move the loop or the ribbon.
10. Cut off any excess wire and insert the wire into the cake.

LEFT: *To create bows and ribbons out of gum paste or fondant, roll the décor medium to ⅛-inch thick and use a ruler or a template to cut out the strips. Use a cutter to create a V shape at each end of the strips. To make a ribbon, attach one end of the strip to a piece of floral wire with a bit of water. To make a bow, fold the strip in half with a piece of floral wire inserted in the middle.*

Fondant Plaques

As used on the Dogwood Cake on page 112.

Cornstarch
Rolling pin
Fondant
Cutters of your choice
Parchment-lined baking sheet
Small offset palette knife

1. Dust the work surface with cornstarch.
2. Roll out the fondant to ⅛ inch or thinner, if desired.
3. Cut out the plaques with the cutters of your choice.
4. Carefully lift the plaques onto the parchment-lined baking sheet using a small offset palette knife.
5. Allow the plaques to dry for 24 hours before decorating.

Fondant Shooting Star Plaque

As used on the Wizard Cake on page 115.

Cornstarch
Blue fondant
Rolling pin
Shooting star template (page 198)
Paring knife
Food color marker

1. Lightly dust the work surface with cornstarch.
2. Roll out the fondant until it is ⅛ inch thick.
3. Cut out the star with the template and a paring knife. Ensure that it is big enough for you to write the inscription.
4. Allow the pieces to dry on parchment paper for 12 to 24 hours.
5. Write the inscription with the food color markers.
6. Use two pearls of the blue fondant to prop the plaque up on the Wizard Cake.

Fondant Tiara

As used on the Castle Cake on page 80.

Cornstarch
Fondant, gum paste, or pastillage
Rolling pin
Tiara template (page 198)
Paring knife
Pink liquid food color
Roller (for stamping)
Tiara stamp
Wide can for shaping the tiara
Icing, food color markers, candies, sanding sugar, nonpareils, and other decorations

1. Slightly dust the work surface with cornstarch.
2. Roll out a piece of décor medium until it is ⅛ inch thick.
3. Place the template on top of the décor medium and cut out the tiara.
4. Use a roller to spread the pink food color onto the stamp. Gently press the stamp onto the tiara.
5. Wrap the tiara around a wide can and then remove the can so that the tiara is standing up on its own.
6. Allow the tiara to dry for 24 hours before decorating with the candies and food color markers.

Fondant Plaques for Castle Cake and Stamped Plaques Cake

- Assorted stamps
- White fondant
- Rolling pin
- Pizza wheel or knife
- Ruler to measure the sides of the cake
- Parchment-lined baking sheet
- Acetate sheet or plastic wrap
- Liquid or gel food colors for painting
- Food color markers
- Plastic roller

As shown on pages 181 and 184.

1. You will need 6 plaques to cover each side of a hexagon cake and 4 plaques to cover each side of a square cake. However, it often is a good idea to make several extra plaques in case of breakage.
2. Measure the width and length of the sides of the cake with a ruler so you will know the dimensions of the square plaques.
3. Roll the white fondant into a square ⅛ inch thick. Using a ruler and a pizza wheel, cut out the plaques. Remember to make a couple extra plaques in case of breakage.
4. Use a small or medium-size offset palette knife to carefully transfer the plaques to a parchment-lined baking sheet that has been dusted with cornstarch.
5. Allow the plaques to dry for 24 hours, and then remove any excess cornstarch with a pastry brush before decorating.
6. Paint or stamp the plaques with food colors or decorate with candy.

VARIATION:

Before allowing the plaques to dry, press the stamp of your choice into the soft fondant. Once the fondant is dry, you can paint the design with liquid or gel food colors.

Fondant Plaque for Painted Hydrangea Garden Cake

- Rolling pin
- White fondant
- Round cookie cutter
- Offset palette knife
- Parchment-lined baking sheet
- Cornstarch
- Piping gel

As shown on page 169.

1. Roll the fondant to ⅛-inch thick, and cut out a plaque with the round cookie cutter.
2. Carefully transfer the plaque with an offset palette knife to a parchment-lined baking sheet that has been dusted with cornstarch.
3. Allow the plaque to dry for 24 hours, and then remove any excess cornstarch with a pastry brush before decorating.
4. Use piping gel to write an inscription on the plaque.

Using Plunger Cutters

Plunger cutters come in many shapes and styles, not just flowers. They make quick decorations and having a few cutters on hand is great for decorating in a pinch.

1. Roll out just enough fondant or gum paste to make small batches of flowers at a time. Dust the work surface with cornstarch or confectioners' sugar and roll out a piece of fondant or gum paste until it is ⅛-inch thick. Keep the piece of décor medium covered with plastic wrap.
2. Lightly dust the foam with cornstarch so that the flowers do not stick. Place the fondant on top of the foam, then place the mouth of the cutter on top of the fondant. Gently push down on the plunger into the foam and lift up. The flower will be released onto the foam already shaped.
3. Repeat this process to create as many flowers as needed. Periodically transfer the flowers to the parchment-lined baking sheet.
4. Allow the flowers to dry for 24 hours.

Fondant or gum paste

Cornstarch or confectioners' sugar

Rolling pin

Plastic wrap

Piece of foam

Plunger cutters (daisies, hearts, etc.)

Parchment-lined baking sheet

VARIATION:

To make the flowers more realistic, pipe pale yellow centers into each flower once they are dry.

Cornstarch

Rolling pin

Gum paste or pastillage

Plastic wrap

Pizza wheel or knife

Parchment-lined baking sheet

Set of heart-shaped cutters

Paring knife

Pastry bag fitted with a #1 tip

White royal icing

Gum Paste or Pastillage Heart Box

As used on the Blush Pink Hearts and Roses Cake on page 106.

1. Dust the work surface with cornstarch. Roll out half of the gum paste or pastillage to just under ⅛-inch thick. Use the largest cutter to cut out two hearts. These will be the base and the top of the box. Transfer the excess décor medium into an air-tight bag or cover with plastic wrap so it does not dry out.

2. Transfer the base and top to a very flat parchment-lined baking sheet or a flat, smooth wooden surface such as a cutting board. Allow them to dry for 24 hours.

3. Dust the work surface with cornstarch and roll out a piece of gum paste or pastillage until it is 1⁄16-inch thick. Use the pizza wheel to cut out a strip of décor medium approximately 1 inch wide. Store the excess pastillage or gum paste in an air-tight bag.

4. On the same parchment-lined baking sheet as the heart base, wrap the pastillage strip around the heart cutter that is two sizes smaller than the cutter used to make the base. Trim the excess décor medium with a small paring knife. This will be the center of the box and will give it height.

5. Gently remove the heart-shaped cutter so that the pastillage strip is standing on its own. Allow the strip to dry for 24 hours.

6. Roll a piece of gum paste or pastillage until it is 1⁄16 inch thick. Cut out a heart with the smallest of the three heart-shaped cutters. Attach this piece to the center of the lid with water or royal icing. Allow the lid to dry.

7. Once all the pieces are dry, pipe a thin line of white royal icing around the edge of the center piece and attach it to the center of the larger heart. Allow it to dry for about 15 minutes. The box is now ready for decoration.

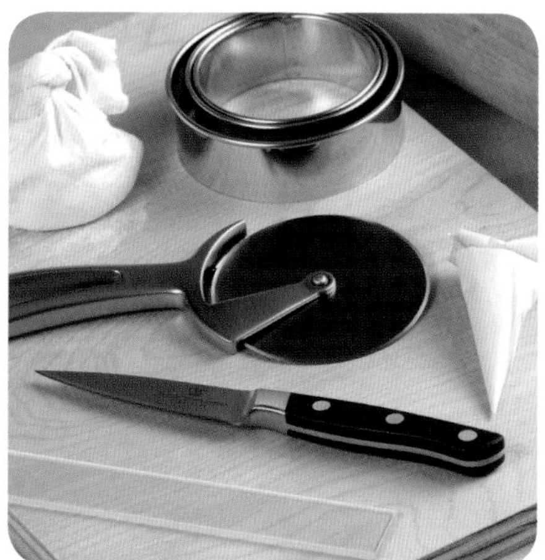

BELOW, LEFT: *Cornstarch pouch, circle cutters, cornet, paring knife, ruler or Plexiglas strip as a cutting guide, pizza wheel.* CENTER: *Use the largest cutter to make the base and the lid of the gift box; the smallest cutter will make the center portion of the lid; use the medium-sized cutter to shape the strip that will form the sides of the gift box.* RIGHT: *Pastillage gift boxes decorated with piping, royal icing floodwork, hand paintings, and pastillage cutouts.*

Gum Paste Quilled Paisleys

Quilling is traditionally done with strips of colorful paper. However, this technique translates nicely into cake decorating by using strips of gum paste or fondant to create flowers, butterflies, and abstract designs. To facilitate the cutting process, cut a strip of cardboard to the length and width that you want your décor medium strips to be and use it as a template. As used on the Quilled Paisley Cake on page 145.

- Cornstarch
- Gum paste, assorted colors
- Rolling pin
- Cardboard strip as a template
- Pizza wheel or a sharp knife
- Plastic wrap
- Water
- Parchment-lined baking sheet

1. Dust the work surface with cornstarch. Roll out the décor medium until it is ⅛ inch thick.
2. Use the cardboard template to cut out strips of gum paste. Cover the gum paste with a piece of plastic wrap.
3. To create the paisleys, fold over one strip of gum paste and connect the two ends of the strip with a bit of water. Work with one color at a time.
4. Wrap a longer strip around the center piece and connect it at the base with a drop of water. Continue building up the paisley using slightly longer strips of gum paste for each new layer.
5. Transfer the paisley to the parchment-lined baking sheet and dry for 24 hours.

AT RIGHT: *Roll out and cut strips of gum paste. To create the paisley shapes, fold over one strip of gum paste and connect the two ends of the strip with a bit of water. Wrap a larger strip around the center piece and connect it at the base. Continue building up the teardrop using slightly larger strips of gum paste for each new layer.*

Gum Paste Quilled Daisy

Cornstarch

White gum paste

Rolling pin

Cardboard strip as a template

Pizza wheel or sharp knife

Plastic wrap

Water

Parchment-lined baking sheet

Yellow gum paste

1. Dust the work surface with cornstarch. Roll the white gum paste until it is ⅛ inch thick.

2. Use the cardboard template to cut out 6 strips of gum paste ⅛ to ¼ inch wide. Cover the gum paste with plastic wrap.

3. Working with one strip of gum paste at a time, wrap the strip around into a loop and secure the ends together with a little bit of water. Try not to pinch the ends as this will distort the shape of the petal.

4. Repeat this process with the remaining 5 petals. Allow the petals to dry, facing upward, on a parchment-lined baking sheet for 24 hours.

5. To make the center of the daisy, take a small amount of yellow gum paste and form a ball. Flatten the ball into a disk and dry for 24 hours on a parchment-lined baking sheet.

6. Arrange the petals on the cake and attach the center with a dot of royal icing. If the daisy must stand up, attach the petals together with royal icing and then attach the center on top. Allow the flower to dry for a minimum of 12 hours.

Chocolate Cutouts

With this simple technique, you can produce a wide variety of cutout chocolate garnishes with a minimal amount of effort.

Tempered chocolate or coating chocolate, melted (see pages 44–45 for chocolate tempering techniques)

Double boiler

Sheet of acetate, chocolate transfer sheet, or page protector

Cutters, such as cookie cutters

Large and small offset palette knives

Parchment-lined baking sheet

1. Prepare the tempered chocolate or melt the coating chocolate in a double boiler over gently simmering water.
2. Spread the chocolate in a thin, even layer (about ¼ inch thick) over the piece of acetate. Allow the chocolate to begin to set and then cut out the shapes with the cutters. If the chocolate has not set enough, the cutter will not create a clean line through the chocolate.
3. Allow the chocolate to set completely. If you want the plaques to be completely flat, tape the sides of the piece of acetate to the work surface before spreading the chocolate.
4. Carefully peel the chocolate cutouts off of the acetate. Do not touch the surfaces of the chocolate cutouts because your fingers will cause smudges.
5. Use the small offset palette knife to transfer the chocolate cutouts to a parchment-lined baking sheet.

AT RIGHT: *To make chocolate garnishes, tempered chocolate and coating chocolate work well. Allowing garnishes to set on acetate and page protectors will give them a shiny finish. Garnishes must be shaped or cut out just before the chocolate sets so they hold the shape but do not crack or break. Coating chocolate comes in various colors and chocolate food colors can also be purchased to transform the appearance of white chocolate.*

Chocolate Curls

Tempered chocolate or melted coating chocolate (see pages 44–45)

Double boiler

Sheet of acetate, chocolate transfer sheet, or page protector

Large offset palette knife

Pizza wheel or knife

Tape

Chocolate curls are a simple and elegant way to garnish a cake. They can be made from different kinds of chocolate, used individually or in combination with other decorations on the same cake. A chocolate transfer sheet has a design printed on it that transfers to the chocolate once the chocolate has set. They can be purchased at online cake decorating stores. Alternatively, cocoa butter or white chocolate can be melted and colored with oil-based food coloring, as explained in the directions at right. Tempered chocolate or coating chocolate is then spread over the top and the curls are cut out and allowed to completely set.

1. Temper the chocolate or melt the coating chocolate using a double boiler set over gently simmering water.
2. Spread a thin layer of chocolate over the acetate with the palette knife.
3. Allow the chocolate to begin to set.
4. Using the pizza wheel, cut the chocolate into triangles. Work quickly so that the chocolate does not set before you have a chance to cut the shapes.
5. Roll the acetate up from corner to corner and tape it closed to prevent it from unrolling.
6. Allow the curls to completely set.
7. Once the chocolate has set, carefully peel the acetate away from the curls.

BELOW, LEFT: *When making chocolate curls, spread a thin layer of tempered chocolate or coating chocolate onto a sheet of acetate; after cutting the chocolate into triangles (working quickly before the chocolate sets), gently roll the strip of acetate into a loose tube and hold it together in this shape with two pieces of tape.* RIGHT: *Once the chocolate has completely set, carefully peel away the acetate from the curls.*

Chocolate Tiles

Dark chocolate or melted coating chocolate (see pages 44–45)

Cocoa butter or melted white chocolate

Double boiler

Oil-based food colors

Sheet of acetate, chocolate transfer sheet, or page protector

Large offset palette knife

Ruler or cardboard template as a guide

Pizza wheel or knife

You will need oil-based food colors for this project because liquid and gel colors are water-based and will not mix with the chocolate.

1. Temper the dark chocolate or melt the coating chocolate. Keep the chocolate fluid so it will be spreadable. This can be accomplished by periodically flashing the chocolate over a hot water bath.
2. Gently melt the cocoa butter or white chocolate in a double boiler. Allow it to cool slightly and color with the food coloring.
3. Fill paper cornets with the colored cocoa butter or white chocolate and create a design over the piece of marble or acetate. If you are using acetate, tape the sheet to the work surface so the tiles do not curl as they set.
4. Pour some of the dark chocolate into the center of the acetate sheet and spread it thinly on top of the cocoa butter with an offset palette knife. Add more chocolate if necessary to obtain an even coating.
5. Once the chocolate is almost set, cut it into equal sized tiles using a ruler or a cardboard template. Begin by cutting strips one way and then cutting in the opposite direction.
6. Allow the tiles to set completely and then lift them off of the acetate.

BELOW, LEFT: *Gently melt the cocoa butter or white chocolate in a double boiler; allow it to cool slightly and color it with oil-based food coloring; fill paper cornets with the colored cocoa butter or white chocolate and create a design over the piece of acetate or marble.* **CENTER:** *Spread an even layer of tempered chocolate or coating chocolate over the cocoa butter or white chocolate design using an offset palette knife.* **RIGHT:** *Once the tiles are almost set, use a ruler or a template to cut out the tiles with a sharp knife.*

Plaques for Cupcakes

Fondant or chocolate plaques are a fun and simple way to decorate cupcakes for any occasion. Use different cutters to represent the theme of your party on your cupcakes, such as hearts for Valentine's Day, shamrocks for St. Patrick's Day, and stars for the Fourth of July.

Pumpkin Plaques

Cornstarch
Rolling pin
White fondant
Pumpkin cutter
Parchment-lined baking sheet
Small offset palette knife
Food color markers, orange and green, or gel colors
Clean, food-safe paint brush

These fondant plaques are shown decorating the top row of Holiday Cupcakes pictured on page 191. You can substitute different cutters to customize these plaques for any project.

1. Dust the work surface lightly with cornstarch. Roll out a piece of fondant to ⅛-inch thick. Cut out the pumpkins with the cutter.
2. Transfer the pumpkins to the baking sheet with a small offset palette knife.
3. Allow the pumpkins to dry for 24 hours.
4. Draw or paint the orange lines onto the pumpkins. Color the stems green.

Reindeer Plaques

Cornstarch
Rolling pin
White fondant
Circle cutter
Blue powdered food color (shimmery or matte)
Plastic wrap
Reindeer stencil
Tamping brush
Small offset palette knife
Parchment-lined baking sheet
Brown liquid or gel food color
Dry, food-safe paint brush

These fondant plaques are shown adorning the bottom row of Holiday Cupcakes pictured on page 191.

1. Dust the work surface lightly with cornstarch. Roll out a piece of fondant until it is ⅛-inch thick. Cut out the plaques with a circle cutter.
2. Lightly dust some blue powdered color around each plaque. Cover the plaques with plastic wrap to prevent them from drying.
3. Place the reindeer stencil on the plaque and use the tamping brush to imprint the reindeer into the soft fondant. Repeat with the remaining plaques.
4. Transfer the plaques to the parchment-lined baking sheet with the small offset palette knife.
5. Allow the plaques to dry for 24 hours.
6. Paint the reindeers with the brown food color. (Paint red noses on them to make Rudolphs!)

Chocolate Heart Plaques

These chocolate plaques are shown atop the middle row of Holiday Cupcakes pictured on page 191.

Tempered chocolate or coating chocolate: dark, milk, or white (see pages 44–45)

Sheet of acetate or a page protector

Tape

Large and small offset palette knives

Heart-shaped cutter

Piping bag fitted with a #1 tip or a paper cornet for piping the inscription

1. Secure the sides of the acetate to the work surface with tape so that the plaques do not curl as they set.
2. Spread the chocolate thinly and evenly over the acetate with the large offset palette knife. Allow the chocolate to begin to set.
3. Cut out the hearts with the cutter.
4. Allow the chocolate to completely set.
5. Peel the hearts off of the acetate.
6. Fill a piping bag or cornet two-thirds full with white chocolate. Pipe an inscription onto each heart.

Embossed Monograms for Adult Cupcakes

These monogrammed fondant plaques top the Embossed Monogram Cupcakes pictured on page 187.

Cornstarch

Rolling pin

Light blue fondant

Fluted oval cutter

Letter stamp, embosser, or stencil

Parchment-lined baking sheet

Small offset palette knife

1. Dust the work surface with cornstarch. Roll the fondant until it's ⅛ inch thick.
2. Cut out the plaques with an oval cutter.
3. Press the letter stamp or the embosser gently into the center of each plaque. If you have a letter stencil, use a tamping brush to transfer the design to the soft fondant.
4. Transfer the plaques to the parchment-lined baking sheet with the small offset palette knife.
5. Allow the plaques to dry for 24 hours.

Chocolate Silhouette

Picture of silhouette

Rectangular, clear, plastic take-out container top

Paper cornets

Dark chocolate, tempered or coating chocolate

White chocolate, tempered or coating chocolate

As used in the decoration of the Silhouette Cake on page 151.

1. Place the picture of the silhouette underneath the plastic container. Fill a paper cornet two-thirds full with dark chocolate. Pipe the outline of the silhouette and then fill it in with the chocolate. Allow the chocolate to set.

2. Fill a paper cornet two-thirds full with white chocolate. Pipe a rectangular outline around the silhouette and fill it in. (This will cover the set silhouette.) Allow the white chocolate to set.

3. Fill a new paper cornet two-thirds full with dark chocolate and fill in the remaining space around the silhouette. Cover the top of the silhouette with chocolate so that the image will have a flat backing of dark chocolate.

4. Allow the chocolate to set and remove the entire piece from the container. It is easier to chill in the freezer for approximately 3 to 5 minutes before unmolding.

BELOW AND OPPOSITE, LEFT TO RIGHT: *Place a picture of a silhouette underneath a clear, plastic container and pipe the silhouette inside the container with dark chocolate. Pipe a rectangular outline around the silhouette with white chocolate and then fill it in so that the silhouette is covered; allow the white chocolate to set. Fill in the remaining space around the silhouette with dark chocolate and cover*

Chocolate Stand

As used in the decoration of the Silhouette Cake on page 151, this stand is used to hold the Chocolate Silhouette on the preceding page in place atop the cake. For contrast, try using milk chocolate for the stand, as shown in the photo on page 152.

Tempered chocolate or coating chocolate

Short jelly-roll pan or 9 × 9-inch brownie pan

Chocolate stand template, page 200; best transferred onto a piece of cardboard rather than paper

Knife

1. Pour the tempered chocolate or the melted coating chocolate into a jelly roll pan or a brownie pan. The chocolate should be about ⅛ inch thick.
2. Allow the chocolate to set almost completely.
3. Place the template on top of the chocolate and cut out the first piece of the stand with a knife. To facilitate cutting, warm the knife by dipping it into hot water and then dry it with a cloth.
4. Repeat with the second piece of the stand.
5. If the edges are a bit rough, pipe a pearl dot border around the edges of the stand with chocolate.

the top of the silhouette so that the image will have a flat backing of dark chocolate. Once the chocolate is completely set, remove the silhouette from the container; wear cloth or latex gloves, if available, as they will prevent your hands from smudging the chocolate. For embellishment, pipe a pearl dot border around the edges of the silhouette with tempered chocolate or melted coating chocolate.

Stenciling with Confectioners' Sugar or Cocoa Powder

The best stencils for dusting are made of thin plastic and can be found at any arts and crafts store in a variety of shapes and designs. A plastic stencil is thicker than one cut out of parchment and will prevent the sugar or cocoa powder from slipping underneath the stencil and smudging the design. A parchment stencil works well if you want to dust sugar or cocoa over an uniced cake, such as a coffee cake. For a colored image, stir powdered food coloring into the confectioners' sugar.

1. To begin, place the stencil on the cake or piece of décor medium, ensuring that there are no gaps between the stencil and the surface being stenciled. You may need to press the stencil down lightly, but be careful not to indent the décor medium.
2. To dust the design, use a very small, fine-meshed sifter or a bag of cheesecloth that has been filled with the sugar or cocoa powder. With the sifter or cheesecloth bag a few inches above the décor medium, dust directly on top of the stencil, making small motions with your hand to ensure that the sugar or cocoa is not dusted outside of the stencil area. Fill the stencil with a very thin layer of sugar or cocoa so that when you remove the stencil there is no excess powder that might spread.
3. Once you have finished dusting, carefully remove the stencil. Beginning at the top, slowly peel the stencil away from the surface of the décor medium as if removing a sticker. Clean and dry the stencil thoroughly before using it again.

Projects

SERVES 10 TO 12

Gift Wrapped Cake

PREPARATION TIMELINE

- **UP TO 2 WEEKS IN ADVANCE:** Prepare gum paste bow
- **UP TO 1 WEEK IN ADVANCE:** Prepare fondant plaque
- **UP TO 2 DAYS IN ADVANCE:** Cover cake board in fondant if not using a cake plate
- **UP TO 2 DAYS IN ADVANCE:** Bake cake
- **UP TO 2 DAYS IN ADVANCE:** Fill and mask cake and cover cake with fondant
- **UP TO 1 DAY IN ADVANCE OR DAY OF EVENT:** Decorate cake

OPPOSITE: *A terrific birthday party cake that resembles a brightly colored present with a large, two-toned bow*

Components

One 8-inch round cake, filled and masked with buttercream and covered with fondant

Two-toned gum paste bow (see Gum Paste or Fondant Bows and Ribbons, page 126)

Multi-coloreed fondant circles

Fondant Plaque (see Fondant Plaques, page 127)

Pearl dot border

Equipment and Materials

CAKE ASSEMBLY

1½ pounds green fondant

Fondant smoothers

Knife

Rolling pin

Cornstarch

Large offset palette knife

GUM PASTE BOW

½ pound gum paste, half green and half blue

Pizza wheel or sharp knife

Cotton balls to shape bow

Cornstarch pouch for dusting

White floral wire (one piece for each loop and ribbon)

White floral tape

Crimping wheel

FONDANT CIRCLES

4 ounces each blue, green, yellow, and orange fondant

Round cutter set (or square, triangle, hearts, etc.)

Rolling pin

Cornstarch

Water

White floral wire (one piece for each ribbon and loop)

White floral tape

FONDANT PLAQUE

4 ounces white fondant

Cornstarch

Rolling pin

Food color marker

PEARL DOT BORDER

Piping bag fitted with a coupler and a #2 tip

Green piping gel

Happy Birthday
Parker

VARIATIONS:

Try using cutters in other shapes, such as hearts, triangles, or squares, for the fondant decorations.

CAKE ASSEMBLY

1. Begin by covering the cake with fondant. Roll out the green fondant into a circle ⅛ inch thick that is large enough to completely enrobe the cake. Dust the fondant lightly with cornstarch and roll the piece of fondant around a rolling pin. Drape the fondant over the cake and smooth the top, edges, and sides with the palms of your hands or fondant smoothers. Trim the fondant around the edge of the cake and remove any bubbles that form in the fondant with a small pin. (See pages 53–55 for cake covering techniques.)

2. Transfer the cake to the desired cake board or cake plate using a large offset spatula to help you ease the cake into the center of the serving dish. If you want to cover the cake board in fondant or royal icing, do so 24 hours before assembly. (See pages 48–49 for cake board-covering techniques.)

3. Refrigerate the cake, covered in plastic wrap, until you are ready to decorate.

FINISHING

1. Roll out different colors of fondant, one color at a time, and cut out different sized circles.

2. Vary the appearance of the circles. Leave some of the circles whole and use a slightly smaller cutter to cut out the centers of some of the others. Cut out sections of a circle with a cutter and then use another circle to fit into the cut-out section. You can use piping tips to cut out different sized dots, as well.

3. Brush a small amount of water onto the backs of the circles and arrange them on the cake.

4. Insert the wire of the two-toned bow into the cake so that it stands up.

5. Write an inscription on the plaque with the food color marker and position the plaque on the cake.

6. Using the pastry bag fitted with a #2 tip and filled with green piping gel pipe a green pearl border around the base of the cake.

SERVES 12 TO 16

Quilled Paisley Cake

Components

One 8-inch square cake, filled and masked with buttercream and covered with fondant

Quilled paisleys (see Gum Paste Quilled Paisleys, page 131)

Fondant plaque with quilled name

Equipment and Materials

CAKE ASSEMBLY

1½ pounds white fondant

Fondant smoothers

Knife

Rolling pin

Cornstarch

Large offset palette knife

QUILLED PAISLEYS

1 pound gum paste in assorted colors

Pizza wheel or a sharp knife

Rolling pin

Cornstarch

Cardboard strip as a template

Water

Parchment-lined baking sheet for drying

PREPARATION TIMELINE

- **UP TO 1 WEEK IN ADVANCE:** Prepare gum paste quilled paisleys
- **UP TO 1 WEEK IN ADVANCE:** Prepare fondant plaque
- **UP TO 2 DAYS IN ADVANCE:** Cover cake board in fondant if not using a cake plate
- **UP TO 2 DAYS IN ADVANCE:** Bake cake
- **UP TO 2 DAYS IN ADVANCE:** Fill and mask cake and cover cake with fondant
- **UP TO 1 DAY IN ADVANCE OR DAY OF EVENT:** Decorate cake

OVERLEAF: *The Quilled Paisley Cake features brightly colored quilled paisleys and a personalized quilled plaque.*

CORY

CAKE ASSEMBLY

1. Begin by covering the cake with fondant. Roll the fondant into a square ¼ inch thick that is large enough to completely enrobe the cake. Dust the fondant lightly with cornstarch and roll the piece of fondant around a rolling pin. Drape the fondant over the cake and smooth the edges with the palms of your hands or fondant smoothers. Trim the fondant around the edge of the cake and remove any bubbles that form in the fondant with a small pin. (See pages 53–55 for cake covering techniques.)
2. Transfer the cake to the desired cake board or cake plate using a large offset spatula to help you ease the cake into the center of the serving dish. If you want to cover the cake board in fondant or royal icing, do so 24 hours before assembly. (See pages 48–49 for cake board-covering techniques.)
3. Refrigerate the cake, covered in plastic wrap, until you are ready to decorate.

FINISHING

1. Secure the dried quilled paisleys to the cake with a small amount of royal icing. You do not want any icing to show. Use a dry, clean brush to remove any excess royal icing. A wet brush will leave a mark on the fondant.
2. Secure the dried fondant plaque to the cake. The inscription can either be piped or quilled.

VARIATIONS:

The quilling technique can be used to make flowers, holiday themed pieces, and abstract designs.

Glazed Cake

SERVES 10 TO 12

PREPARATION TIMELINE

- **UP TO 2 DAYS IN ADVANCE:** Cover cake board in fondant if not using a cake plate
- **UP TO 2 DAYS IN ADVANCE:** Bake cake
- **UP TO 1 DAY IN ADVANCE:** Fill cake with choice of icing
- **UP TO 1 DAY IN ADVANCE:** (up to 3 days in advance, if using tempered chocolate) Prepare chocolate tiles
- **UP TO 1 DAY IN ADVANCE:** Glaze cake with chocolate glaze
- **UP TO 1 DAY IN ADVANCE OR DAY OF EVENT:** Decorate cake

OPPOSITE: *A ganache-covered cake with multi-color chocolate tiles*

Components

One 8-inch round cake, filled and glazed (see Glazing a Cake with Ganache, page 56, for method)

Rectangular chocolate tiles (see Chocolate Tiles, page 135, for method)

Equipment and Materials

CHOCOLATE TILES

Dark chocolate or melted coating chocolate

Cocoa butter or melted white chocolate

Double boiler

Oil-based food colors

Sheet of acetate or page protector

Large offset palette knife

Ruler or cardboard template as a guide

Pizza wheel or knife

Paper cornet or piping bag fitted with a #1 tip for the inscription, if desired

FINISHING

1. Arrange the tiles around the glazed cake, pressing them gently to adhere to the glaze. They can either lie flat against the cake or be placed at a slight angle as shown.

2. Pipe an inscription on the top of the cake in ganache, chocolate, or piping gel if desired.

VARIATIONS:

Chocolate curls or marzipan fruit look very elegant on glazed cakes. A plaque could be made out of chocolate or fondant for writing an inscription.

Silhouette Cake

Components

One 8-inch round cake, filled and masked with buttercream, and covered with fondant

Chocolate piping gel fleur-de-lis and pearl dot border

Chocolate silhouette (see Chocolate Silhouette, page 138, for method)

Chocolate stand (see Chocolate Stand, page 139, for method)

Equipment and Materials

CAKE ASSEMBLY

1½ pounds chocolate fondant

Rolling pin

Fondant smoothers

Knife

Small pin

Large offset palette knife

FLEUR-DE-LIS

Piping bag fitted with a coupler and a #1 tip or a paper cornet

Chocolate piping gel (page 40)

PEARL DOT BORDER

Piping bag fitted with a coupler and a #1 tip or a paper cornet

Chocolate piping gel (page 40)

CHOCOLATE SILHOUETTE

Picture of silhouette

Rectangular, clear, plastic take-out container

Paper cornets

Dark chocolate, tempered or coating chocolate

White chocolate, tempered or coating chocolate

CHOCOLATE STAND

Tempered chocolate or coating chocolate

Short jelly-roll pan or 9 × 9-inch brownie pan

Chocolate stand template, page 200; best transferred onto a piece of cardboard rather than paper

Knife

PREPARATION TIMELINE

- **UP TO 2 DAYS IN ADVANCE:** Cover cake board in fondant
- **UP TO 2 DAYS IN ADVANCE:** Bake cake
- **UP TO 2 DAYS IN ADVANCE:** Fill and mask cake and cover cake with fondant
- **UP TO 1 DAY IN ADVANCE:** (up to 3 days in advance, if using tempered chocolate) Prepare chocolate silhouette and stand
- **UP TO 1 DAY IN ADVANCE OR DAY OF EVENT:** Decorate cake

CAKE ASSEMBLY

1. Dust the work surface with confectioners' sugar. Roll the chocolate fondant into a circle ⅜-inch thick. Dust the fondant lightly with confectioners' sugar and roll the piece of fondant around a rolling pin. Drape the fondant over the cake and smooth the edges with the palms of your hands or with the fondant smoothers. Trim the fondant around the edge of the cake and remove any bubbles that form in the fondant with a small pin (see pages 53–55 for cake covering techniques). Brush off any excess confectioners' sugar with a pastry brush.

2. Transfer the cake to the desired cake board or cake plate using a large offset palette knife to help you ease the cake into the center of the serving dish. If you want to cover the cake board in fondant or royal icing, do so 24 hours before assembly (see pages 48–49 for cake board covering techniques).

FINISHING

1. Make the chocolate silhouette and allow it to set. Remove it from the plastic container. Do not handle the silhouette too much because your fingers will smudge the chocolate.

2. Make the chocolate stand. Attach the two sides together with tempered chocolate or coating chocolate.

3. Pipe the fleur-de-lis around the sides of the cake with the piping gel, spacing them out evenly. Pipe a pearl dot border around the base of the cake. Pipe a loop design on the top of the cake, close to the edge.

4. Secure the stand to the cake with more tempered or coating chocolate.

5. Place the silhouette in the stand. You can secure it to the stand with additional chocolate if desired.

OPPOSITE: *The Silhouette Cake, with chocolate silhouette and chocolate piping gel fleur-de-lis*

MAKES 24 CUPCAKES

Chocolate Flower Cupcakes

PREPARATION TIMELINE

- UP TO 3 DAYS IN ADVANCE: Make the flowers
- UP TO 1 DAY IN ADVANCE: Make the cupcakes
- DAY OF EVENT: Decorate the cupcakes

Components

Cupcakes

Equipment and Materials

Dark modeling chocolate

White modeling chocolate

Oil-based food colors

Large and medium flower cutters

Tempered or coating chocolate

Teacups or small bowls for shaping flowers

Small circle cutter

Hard ganache for glazing

ASSEMBLY

1. Roll out the dark modeling chocolate until it is ⅛-inch thick.
2. Cut out the desired number of large flowers.
3. Place the flowers over the bottoms of inverted teacups or inside the small bowls. They will need to dry for 12 to 24 hours.
4. Cut out as many small circles from the dark modeling chocolate as there will be flowers. These circles will be the centers of the flowers.
5. Tint the white modeling chocolate pink using the oil-based food colors. Repeat steps 1 through 3 with the pink modeling chocolate and the medium-sized flower cutter.
6. Once the components are dry, secure the pink flowers inside the larger chocolate flowers with a small amount of water.
7. Secure a dark modeling chocolate center inside each flower with a small amount of water.

FINISHING

1. Dip each cupcake into the fluid hard ganache.
2. Place a flower on top of each cupcake. Once the ganache sets, the flowers will be secured to the cupcakes.

OPPOSITE: *Chocolate cupcakes dipped in fluid hard ganache and decorated with two-toned modeling chocolate flowers*

PREPARATION TIMELINE

- **UP TO 3 DAYS IN ADVANCE:** Prepare chocolate tiles
- **UP TO 2 DAYS IN ADVANCE:** Cover cake board in fondant
- **UP TO 2 DAYS IN ADVANCE:** Bake cake
- **UP TO 1 DAY IN ADVANCE:** Fill and ice cake with buttercream
- **UP TO 1 DAY IN ADVANCE OR DAY OF EVENT:** Decorate cake

OPPOSITE: *A buttercream-iced cake decorated with a mosaic design in blue- and green-colored chocolate tiles*

Components

One 11 × 15-inch rectangle cake, filled and iced with pale green buttercream

½-inch × ½-inch green and blue tiles (see Chocolate Tiles, page 135, for method)

Equipment and Materials

CAKE ASSEMBLY

Regular and offset palette knives for icing the cake

Pale green buttercream

TILES

White chocolate or melted coating chocolate

Double boiler

Oil-based food colors

Sheet of acetate or page protector

Large offset palette knife

Ruler or cardboard template as a guide

Pizza wheel or knife

CAKE ASSEMBLY AND FINISHING

1. Begin by icing the cake with your choice of buttercream. The technique is the same as for masking a cake; however, you will use more buttercream so that no parts of the cake can be seen (see pages 53–55 for icing techniques).

2. Prepare the tiles based on a mosaic pattern of your choice.

3. Arrange the tiles on the top and sides of the cake. Coating chocolate tiles can be easily cut with a paring knife to create your mosaic design. Be sure to cut the tiles in a way so that the design will extend to the very bottom of the cake.

VARIATIONS:

Look on the Internet and in books for beautiful mosaic tile patterns. Try different color combinations for the tiles.

Chapter Nine

Embossing, Stamping, and Painting

EMBOSSING, STAMPING, AND painting are fun and simple techniques that are great for decorating projects with children. They require very little equipment and it all can be purchased inexpensively at craft or cake decorating stores. Embossing creates a raised design on the surface of the cake or on a décor medium plaque, so it is important to use them when the fondant, marzipan, or modeling chocolate is still soft so it does not crack. A tamping brush and a stencil, both of which can be purchased at craft stores, can be used to create a design on the décor medium.

There are limitless options when it comes to stamping, because hundreds of images and designs are available in stamp form at craft and hobby stores. One method is to press the stamp into the soft décor medium and then allow it to dry. The image can be painted with food color once the piece is completely dry. A stamp can be lightly dipped in liquid food color and then gently pressed against a fondant-covered cake or onto a dry décor medium plaque. For a cake decorator who is not comfortable hand painting a design or image on a cake, a stamp is a great alternative. Designs similar to those created by stamps can be made with objects found around the house, such as shaped pins, buttons, or pieces of costume jewelry.

To paint on a fondant cake, all you need is food color and a clean paint brush, available at any art store. To paint with powdered food color or luster powders, a clear liquid, such as lemon extract or vodka, must be mixed into the powder. Dried gum paste or fondant flowers can be painted or dusted with powdered food color to make them appear more realistic. Royal icing garnishes and borders can also be painted. Royal icing is very fragile when dry so it is important to have a light touch. Painting works well with embossed designs that sometimes need a bit of color to draw more attention to them. Finally, sponge painting onto the side of a cake creates texture as well as color and will be a hit with adults and children alike.

LEFT *Embossed, painted, and stamped plaques are simple and attractive cake decorations. These techniques can also be applied directly onto a cake that has been covered in décor medium.*

OPPOSITE, LEFT: *Dip a plastic roller into liquid food color and then spread the color over the stamp; this technique will apply just enough color to the stamp and will prevent smudging.* **CENTER:** *Press the stamp onto the dried décor medium plaque or the side of the cake itself.* **RIGHT:** *Embellish the stamp with designs using food color markers or a paint brush and liquid or gel food colors; allow the plaque to dry completely before using.*

Stamping Images on Fondant Plaques

This technique is used to create the plaques for the Stamped Plaques Cake, page 183.

1. Measure the width and length of the sides of the cake with a ruler so you will know the dimensions that the squares need to be.
2. Roll the fondant into a square ⅛-inch thick. Using a ruler and a pizza wheel, cut out the desired number of plaques. It is usually a good idea to make a couple extra plaques in case of breakage.
3. Transfer the plaques with an offset spatula to a parchment-lined baking sheet that has been dusted with cornstarch.
4. Allow the plaques to dry for 24 hours and remove any excess cornstarch with a dry pastry brush before decorating.
5. Spread a thin layer of liquid food color over a sheet of acetate or a piece of plastic wrap.
6. Roll the plastic roller in the liquid food color and then roll the color onto the stamp. Gently press the stamp onto the dried plaque.
7. Create background images with the food color markers or liquid food colors and paint brushes. Allow the paintings to dry completely.
8. Gently place the finished plaques against the sides of the cake. A buttercream-iced cake should hold the plaques in place; but if doesn't, apply a small amount of fresh buttercream to the backs of the plaques. Use royal icing to attach the plaques to a fondant-covered cake.
9. Pipe the inscription with the colored piping gel.

Ruler to measure the sides of the cake

Fondant

Rolling pin

Plastic roller

Pizza wheel or knife

Parchment-lined baking sheet

Offset spatula

Pastry brush

Liquid or gel food colors for painting

Sheet of acetate or acetate page protector

Stamps

Food color markers

Piping bag fitted with a #2 tip

Colored piping gel for the inscription

Stamping on the Side of a Cake

Liquid food color

Sheet of acetate or a acetate page protector

Stamp of your choice

This very simple technique can be used to create just about any image you want. All you need is a stamp and some food color. This technique was used to make the grass on the Stamped Wildflowers and Butterfly Cake, page 174.

1. Begin by covering your cake with fondant or white modeling chocolate, (see pages 53–55 for cake covering techniques).

2. Spread a thin layer of liquid food coloring on the piece of acetate or the plastic wrap. Dip the plastic roller in the liquid food color and even out the color on the acetate with the roller. Once the color is even, roll the color onto the stamp making sure that the entire stamp has been covered.

3. Gently press the stamp against the side of the cake.

4. The stamp can then be embellished by painting on the cake with food color, by drawing with food color markers, or applying candy or décor medium decorations.

LEFT: To stamp around the base of a cake, lift the cake slightly off of the surface that it is resting on, so that the stamp will be flush with the side of the cake. A bread and butter plate works well for this.

Embossing

Embossing is a simple technique that is quite similar to stamping. This technique is used for the dragon on the Castle Cake, shown on page 181. The embossing tools, which are usually plastic, or stamps can be pressed into soft fondant to create a design. Embossing tools and stamps are both inexpensive and can be found at cake decorating and craft stores.

Embossing tools or stamps

Liquid or gel food color

Clean, food-safe food brush

Food color markers

1. Press the embossing tool or the stamp firmly into the soft fondant.
2. Leave the design as it is or outline the design with a paint brush and food colors or with food color markers. You can paint additional details on and around the embossed design or you can embellish it with piping.

BELOW, LEFT: *Press the stamp or other embossing tool firmly into the soft décor medium; allow the plaque to dry for approximately 24 hours.* **CENTER:** *Outline the embossed design with food color markers or a paint brush and liquid or gel food colors.* **RIGHT:** *If desired, add more color detail to the embossed design with food color markers or a paint brush and liquid or gel food colors.*

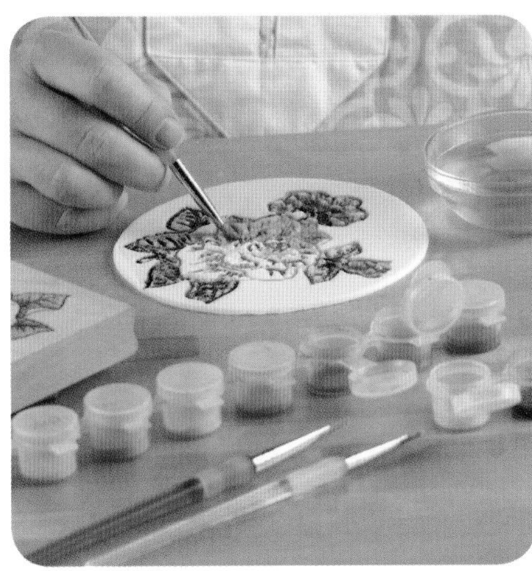

Painting with Food Colors

Nearly anything can be painted onto a cake. Have a picture or the real object in front of you for guidance. You can also use this method for painting on fondant or gum paste plaques or flowers

Painted Flowers

Pink and green, or blue, green, and yellow liquid, gel, or powdered food colors

Clean, food-safe paint brush

This technique is used for the Painted Hydrangea Garden Cake, page 168.

1. Prepare the food coloring to be used as paint. Liquid colors are ready to be used as paints and only need a damp brush. Powdered food colors needs to be mixed with a small amount of vodka or lemon extract. Add just a few drops at a time until the food color has the consistency of watercolor paints. Gel colors need to be thinned out slightly with water or a clear liquor, like vodka.

2. Using a clean brush, paint hydrangeas of various sizes onto the sides of the cake. It is often helpful to have a picture of a hydrangea or a real bouquet of hydrangeas in front of you for guidance. Use the green and yellow food colors to create shading. Try to space the flowers evenly around the cake.

LEFT: *Use a clean paint brush from a craft store and liquid or gel food colors to paint designs on a cake. To paint with powdered food coloring, you will need to add a few drops of liquid to the powder, such as lemon extract.*

Sponge Painting a Fondant Covered Cake

Liquid food coloring

Shallow dish

Dry sea sponge, available at craft stores

This technique is used for the Mermaid Cake, page 171.

1. Pour some liquid food coloring into a shallow dish. Dip a dry sea sponge lightly in the food coloring and remove the excess color by running the sponge along the side of the dish.

2. Dab the sponge onto the side of the cake. Continue until the entire cake is sponged, but you can also see the white fondant coming through the sponged design.

Projects

SERVES 10 TO 12

Painted Hydrangea Garden Cake

PREPARATION TIMELINE

- **UP TO 2 WEEKS IN ADVANCE:** Prepare gum paste hydrangea bouquet
- **UP TO 2 WEEKS IN ADVANCE:** Prepare gum paste bow
- **UP TO 1 WEEK IN ADVANCE:** Prepare fondant plaque
- **UP TO 2 DAYS IN ADVANCE:** Cover cake board in fondant
- **UP TO 2 DAYS IN ADVANCE:** Bake cake
- **UP TO 2 DAYS IN ADVANCE:** Fill and mask cake and cover cake with fondant
- **UP TO 1 DAY IN ADVANCE OR DAY OF EVENT:** Decorate cake

OPPOSITE: *Painted Hydrangea Garden Cake with a gum paste hydrangea bouquet, personalized fondant plaque, a gum paste bow, and hand-painted hydrangeas.*

Components

One 9-inch round cake, filled and masked with buttercream

Gum paste hydrangea bouquet (see Gum Paste Hydrangeas, page 94, for method)

Gum paste bow (see Gum Paste or Fondant Bows and Ribbons, page 126, for method)

Fondant plaque (see Fondant Plaque for Painted Hydrangea Garden Cake, page 128, for method)

Equipment and Materials

CAKE ASSEMBLY

2 pounds fondant, lavender or pale blue

Cornstarch

Rolling pin

Fondant smoothers

Knife

Small pin

Large offset palette knife

HYDRANGEA BOUQUET

½ pound gum paste, pale blue

36 pieces of thin, white floral wire

Small pair of scissors

Floral tape

Thin knitting needle

Small pliers, for shaping the angle of the flowers in the bouquet

Anger tool (a gum paste tool with a cone at the tip)

Ball tool

PAINTED HYDRANGEAS

Blue, green, purple, and yellow liquid, gel, or powdered food colors

Clean paint brush

GUM PASTE BOW

Cornstarch pouch for dusting (see page 38)

Rolling pin

½ pound gum paste

Ruler

Pizza wheel or sharp knife

Water

Cotton balls to shape bow

Parchment-lined baking sheet

White floral wire (one piece for each loop and ribbon)

White floral tape

FONDANT PLAQUE

Ruler

Rolling pin

4 ounces fondant

Offset spatula

Parchment-lined baking sheet

Small offset palette knife

Cutter of your choice

Cornstarch

Food color markers

Happy
Birthday
Eileen

VARIATIONS:

If you do not want to paint flowers on the cake, try sponge painting the colors on the side of the cake instead. This creates an attractive, textured appearance and makes the cake more colorful.

CAKE ASSEMBLY

1. Begin by covering the cake with fondant. Roll the lavender or blue fondant into a circle ⅜-inch thick that is large enough to completely enrobe the cake. Dust the fondant lightly with cornstarch and roll the piece of fondant around a rolling pin. Drape the fondant over the cake and smooth the edges with the palms of your hands or with the fondant smoothers. Trim the fondant around the edge of the cake and remove any bubbles that form in the fondant with a small pin (see pages 53–55 for cake covering techniques).

2. Transfer the cake to the desired cake board or cake plate using a large offset spatula to help you ease the cake into the center of the serving dish. If you want to cover the cake board in fondant or royal icing, do so 24 hours before assembly (see pages 48–49 for cake board-covering techniques.)

3. Refrigerate the cake, covered in plastic wrap, until you are ready to decorate.

FINISHING

1. Prepare the food coloring to paint the hydrangeas and vines. Liquid food colors are ready to be used as paints and only need a damp brush. Powdered food colors must be mixed with a small amount of a clear liquid, such as lemon extract or vodka. Add just a few drops at a time until the food color has the consistency of watercolor paints. Gel food colors must be thinned out slightly with a clear liquid as well.

2. Using a clean brush, paint hydrangeas of various sizes on the sides of the cake. It is often helpful to have a picture of a hydrangea or a real bouquet of hydrangeas in front of you for guidance. Use different shades of blue to create depth and add accents of yellow, purple, and green. Try to evenly space out the flowers around the cake.

3. Insert the stem of the hydrangea bouquet into the cake.

4. Insert the floral wires holding the bow together into the cake next to the hydrangeas.

5. Write an inscription on the plaque with the food color marker and secure the plaque to the cake with a small amount of royal icing.

Mermaid Cake

Components

One 8-inch round cake, filled and masked with buttercream

One 6-inch round cake, filled and masked with buttercream

Chocolate shells (see Chocolate Molds and Chocolate Sea Shells, page 95)

Chocolate mermaid (see sidebar, page 173)

Chocolate wave (see sidebar, page 173)

Fondant bands for each tier (see Fondant, Gum Paste, and Décor Bands, page 124)

Equipment and Materials

CAKE ASSEMBLY

2½ pounds pale blue fondant

7 straws for dowels (see Doweling a Cake, page 57)

Scissors for cutting straw dowels

Fondant smoothers

Knife

Rolling pin

Cornstarch

Large offset palette knife

Blue and green liquid food coloring

2 sea sponges

Royal icing

CHOCOLATE MERMAID

Mermaid template (see page 199)

Tempered white chocolate or coating chocolate (green, white, yellow)

Acetate sheet or page protector

Piping bags or paper cornets fitted with a #1 tip

CHOCOLATE WAVE

Wave template (see page 199)

Tempered white chocolate or coating chocolate (blue)

Acetate sheet or page protector

Piping bag or paper cornet fitted with a #1 tip

FONDANT BANDS

8 ounces white fondant

Plastic, flexible tape measure

Rolling pin

Pizza wheel or knife

Cornstarch

Food color markers

PREPARATION TIMELINE

➡ **UP TO 2 DAYS IN ADVANCE:**
Prepare chocolate shells

➡ **UP TO 2 DAYS IN ADVANCE:**
Prepare chocolate mermaid

➡ **UP TO 2 DAYS IN ADVANCE:**
Prepare chocolate wave

➡ **UP TO 2 DAYS IN ADVANCE:**
Cover cake board in fondant

➡ **UP TO 2 DAYS IN ADVANCE:**
Bake cake

➡ **UP TO 2 DAYS IN ADVANCE:**
Fill and mask cake and cover cake with fondant

➡ **UP TO 2 DAYS IN ADVANCE:**
Assemble cake

➡ **UP TO 1 DAY IN ADVANCE OR DAY OF EVENT:**
Decorate cake

Happy Birthday Emily

CAKE ASSEMBLY

1. Begin by covering the 8-inch cake with fondant. Roll 1½ pounds of white fondant into a circle ¼ inch thick that is large enough to completely enrobe the cake. Dust the fondant lightly with cornstarch and roll the piece of fondant around a rolling pin. Drape the fondant over the cake and smooth the edges with the palm of your hands or with the fondant smoothers. Trim the fondant around the edge of the cake and remove any bubbles that form in the fondant with a small pin. (See page 53–55 for cake covering techniques.) Repeat with the second cake.
2. Spread some royal icing onto the center of the cake board. Transfer the largest cake to the cake board using a large offset palette knife to help you ease the cake into the center of the board.
3. Insert one of the straws into the center of the cake and mark where the straw is flush with the cake. Cut the remaining 6 straws the same height as the first. Insert 5 straws into the cake in a circle and place 2 in the middle of the cake. Use a 6-inch cake pan to help you guide the placement of the straws. (See page 57 for doweling instructions).
4. Dab a small amount of royal icing on top of each dowel. Using a large offset palette knife, place the 6-inch cake on top of the base cake, making sure it is perfectly centered and level. Press the cake down gently so that is secure.
5. Refrigerate the cake until you are ready to decorate.

FINISHING

1. Pour blue and green liquid food coloring into separate shallow dishes. Dip a damp sea sponge lightly into the food coloring remove the excess color by running the sponge along the side of the dish. Dab the sponge onto the side of the cake.
2. Alternate using the green and the blue food coloring, using separate sponges for each color. Continue until the entire cake is sponged, but you can also see the white fondant coming through the color.
3. Once the cake is dry, make the fondant bands and wrap them around the tiers. Write an inscription with food color markers on the band around the 6-inch tier.
4. Secure the mermaid, wave, and shells to the cake with white royal icing.

OPPOSITE: *A two-tiered cake with sponge-painted fondant, chocolate sea shells, and a chocolate mermaid cake topper*

TO MAKE THE CHOCOLATE MERMAID AND CHOCOLATE WAVE:

The method to make the chocolate mermaid as shown on the Mermaid Cake is similar to the Chocolate Silhouette (page 138). Substitute the Mermaid Template (page 199) and a sheet of acetate. Fill three cornets two-thirds full with tempered white chocolate or coating chocolate, two of which have been tinted yellow and green. Pipe the outline following the colors shown on page 172 (yellow for the hair, white for the upper body, and green for the tail), and then fill it in with the corresponding color. Allow to set. Using the cornet of tempered white chocolate or coating chocolate, cover the top of the entire mermaid so the image has a flat backing of white chocolate. Allow the chocolate to set and remove the entire piece from the acetate.

The method to make the chocolate wave is the same as the Chocolate Stand (page 139). Substitute the Wave Template (page 199) and use tempered white chocolate or coating chocolate that has been tinted blue.

SERVES 10 TO 12

Stamped Wildflowers and Butterflies Cake

PREPARATION TIMELINE

- **UP TO 1 WEEK IN ADVANCE:** Prepare fondant daisies
- **UP TO 3 DAYS IN ADVANCE:** Prepare royal icing butterflies
- **UP TO 2 DAYS IN ADVANCE:** Cover cake board in fondant
- **UP TO 2 DAYS IN ADVANCE:** Bake cake
- **UP TO 2 DAYS IN ADVANCE:** Fill and mask cake and cover cake with fondant
- **UP TO 1 DAY IN ADVANCE OR DAY OF EVENT:** Decorate cake

OPPOSITE: *Stamped Wildflowers and Butterflies Cake with stamped grass, fondant flower cutouts, and royal icing butterflies*

Components

One 8-inch round cake, filled and masked with buttercream

Royal icing butterflies (see Royal Icing Butterflies, page 123, for method)

Small fondant daisies (see Using Plunger Cutters, page 129, for method)

Equipment and Materials

CAKE ASSEMBLY

1½ pounds white fondant

Cornstarch

Rolling pin

Fondant smoothers

Knife

Small pin

Large offset palette knife

ROYAL ICING BUTTERFLIES

Butterfly wing template (see page 200)

White royal icing

Small offset palette knife

White flower stamens (see Shopping Resources, page 195)

Plastic or metal bars

FONDANT DAISIES

4 ounces yellow fondant

Cornstarch or confectioners' sugar

Rolling pin

Plastic wrap

Piece of foam

Plunger daisy cutters

Piping bag fitted with #1 tip

White royal icing for centers

GRASS

Green liquid food color

Sheet of acetate or plastic wrap

Roller

Grass stamp

PEARL DOT BORDER

Piping bag fitted with a coupler and a #2 tip

Green piping gel

VARIATIONS

Numerous types of flower and plunger cutters are available.

CAKE ASSEMBLY

1. Begin by covering the cake with fondant. Roll out the white fondant into a circle ⅜-inch thick that is large enough to completely enrobe the cake. Dust the fondant lightly with cornstarch and roll the piece of fondant around a rolling pin. Drape the fondant over the cake and smooth the edges with the palms of your hands or with the fondant smoothers. Trim the fondant around the edge of the cake and remove any bubbles that form in the fondant with a small pin (see pages 53–55 for cake covering techniques).

2. Transfer the cake to the desired cake board or cake plate using a large offset spatula to help you ease the cake into the center of the serving dish. If you want to cover the cake board in fondant or royal icing, do so 24 hours before assembly (see pages 48–49 for cake board-covering techniques).

3. Refrigerate the cake, covered in plastic wrap, until you are ready to decorate.

FINISHING

1. Elevate the cake slightly from the work surface with a small inverted plate. This is done because the stamp has a border around it and you want the grass to begin at the bottom of the cake.

2. Pour some green liquid food coloring onto a sheet of acetate or plastic wrap. Dip the roller in the color and roll it on the plastic until it is evenly coated with color.

3. Roll the color onto the stamp until evenly coated, then press the stamp gently onto the side of the cake. You will have to rock the stamp with steady, even pressure from one side of the stamp to the other because the cake is curved.

4. Pipe centers in the daisies with yellow royal icing and secure them to the cake with royal icing.

5. Secure the butterflies to the cake with royal icing.

Pixie Cake

Components

One 8-inch square cake, filled and masked with buttercream

Fondant plaque stamped with fairy (see Fondant Plaques, page 127)

Equipment and Materials

CAKE ASSEMBLY

1½ pounds ivory or white fondant

Fondant smoothers

Knife

Rolling pin

Cornstarch

Large offset palette knife

GRASS AND FLOWERS

Grass stamp

Food coloring pens or flower stamps

Liquid or gel food colors

Clean paint brush

FAIRY PLAQUE

4 ounces white fondant

Cornstarch

Rolling pin

Pixie bubble template (page 196)

Fairy stamp

Liquid or gel food color

Royal icing and a piping bag or food color marker for the inscription

PREPARATION TIMELINE

- **UP TO 1 WEEK IN ADVANCE:** Prepare fondant plaque
- **UP TO 2 DAYS IN ADVANCE:** Cover cake board in fondant if not using a cake plate
- **UP TO 2 DAYS IN ADVANCE:** Bake cake
- **UP TO 2 DAYS IN ADVANCE:** Fill and mask cake and cover cake with fondant
- **UP TO 1 DAY IN ADVANCE OR DAY OF EVENT:** Paint and decorate cake

Happy Birthday Mia

CAKE ASSEMBLY

1. Begin by covering the cake with fondant. Massage a little blue food coloring into the white fondant to create a marbled effect. Roll out the white fondant into a square ¼ inch thick that is large enough to completely enrobe the cake. Dust the fondant lightly with cornstarch and roll the piece of fondant around a rolling pin. Drape the fondant over the cake and smooth the edges with the palm of your hands or fondant smoothers. Trim the fondant around the edge of the cake and remove any bubbles that form in the fondant with a small pin. (See pages 53–55 for cake covering techniques.)
2. Transfer the cake to the desired cake board or cake plate using a large offset spatula to help you ease the cake into the center of the serving dish. If you want to cover the cake board in fondant or royal icing, do so 24 hours before assembly. (See pages 48–49 for cake board-covering techniques.)
3. Refrigerate the cake, covered in plastic wrap, until you are ready to decorate.

FINISHING

1. Roll the liquid food coloring onto the grass stamp and gently press it against the side of the cake. Continue stamping around the entire base of the cake.
2. Use flower stamps dipped in food coloring to make flowers around the cake, or use food coloring pens to draw the flowers onto the cake.
3. Paint the pixie on the plaque with liquid or gel food coloring.
4. Use royal icing and a piping bag or a food color marker to create the inscription on the plaque.
5. Secure the plaque to the top of the cake with royal icing.

VARIATIONS:

Any combination of stamps can be used to create a different themed cake.

OPPOSITE: *An elegant child's cake with stamped flowers and a personalized, fairy plaque*

SERVES 18 TO 22

Castle Cake

PREPARATION TIMELINE

- **UP TO 3 DAYS IN ADVANCE:** Prepare the castle walls
- **UP TO 3 DAYS IN ADVANCE:** Prepare the tiara
- **UP TO 2 DAYS IN ADVANCE:** Cover cake board in fondant if not using a cake plate
- **UP TO 2 DAYS IN ADVANCE:** Bake cake
- **UP TO 2 DAYS IN ADVANCE:** Fill and ice cake with buttercream
- **UP TO 1 DAY IN ADVANCE OR DAY OF EVENT:** Decorate cake

Components

One 12-inch hexagon cake, filled and iced with pink buttercream

6 fondant castle walls (see Fondant Plaques for Castle Cake and Stamped Plaques Cake, page 128)

Fondant tiara (see Fondant Tiara, page 127)

Fondant plaque for inscription

Equipment and Materials

CAKE ASSEMBLY

Regular and offset palette knives for icing the cake

Pink buttercream

Dark pink, light pink, and white nonpareils for top of cake (see Shopping Resources, page 195)

CASTLE WALLS

1½ pounds white fondant

Rolling pin

Cornstarch

Castle wall template (see page 199)

Dragon stamp

Clean paint brush

Pizza wheel or a knife

Liquid or gel food colors

Food color markers

Colored candy sticks

TIARA

4 ounces white fondant

Tiara template (see page 198)

Rolling pin

Cornstarch

Can for shaping the tiara

Knife

Sanding sugar

Powdered food color (purple, pink, etc.)

Embossing tools (optional)

Parchment paper

Royal icing

Piping bag fitted with a #2 plain tip

FONDANT PLAQUE

4 ounces white fondant

Rolling pin

Cornstarch

Knife

Piping gel and a piping bag or food color marker for the inscription

Happy Birthday Princess Claire

CAKE ASSEMBLY

1. Begin by icing the cake with the blush pink buttercream. The technique is the same as for masking a cake; however you will use more buttercream so that no parts of the cake can be seen. (See page 51–53 for icing techniques).

FINISHING

1. Begin by cutting out the castle walls and the tiara. Dust the work surface with cornstarch. Roll out white fondant to ⅛ inch thick. Using the template and a paring knife, cut out 6 walls. If desired, press a dragon stamp onto one or more of the walls.
2. Place the walls on a parchment-lined baking sheet and allow them to dry for 24 hours.
3. Roll out another piece of white fondant ⅛ inch thick. Using the tiara template and a paring knife, cut out the tiara. This is the time to use any embossing tools to imprint designs into the tiara.
4. Dust the back of the tiara with cornstarch. Wrap the tiara around a can or another round object that had been placed on a piece of parchment paper. Allow the tiara to sit for about 3 minutes. Carefully remove the can and the tiara should stand up on its own. Allow it to dry for 24 hours.
5. Once dry, decorate the walls. Paint the dragon with gel or liquid food colors. Paint trees, doors, and windows onto the plaques with food color or with food color markers. Allow the paintings to dry.
6. Decorate the tiara. Color the sanding sugar by mixing it with powdered food color. Pipe designs on the tiara with white royal icing and then gently press the royal icing into the sanding sugar until it adheres.
7. Gently place the castle walls against the sides of the cake. The buttercream should hold the plaques in place, but if it doesn't, apply a small amount of fresh buttercream to the backs of the plaques.
8. Sprinkle dark pink, light pink, and white nonpareils on the top of the cake to create a stonework effect.
9. Carefully position the tiara on the top of the cake. Use piping gel or a food color marker to create the inscription on the fondant plaque, and position on the cake.

SERVES 10 TO 12

Stamped Plaques Cake

Components

One 8-inch square cake, filled and iced with buttercream

4 stamped fondant plaques (see Fondant Plaques for Castle Cake and Stamped Plaques Cake, page 128, and Stamping Images on Fondant Plaques, page 163)

Fondant figure of boy on a toy truck (see page 103)

Fondant plaque for inscription

Buttercream shell border

Equipment and Materials

CAKE ASSEMBLY

Regular and offset palette knives for icing the cake

White buttercream

FONDANT PLAQUES

1 pound white fondant

Rolling pin

Cornstarch

Pizza wheel or knife

Ruler to measure the sides of the cake

Parchment-lined baking sheet

Acetate sheet or plastic wrap

Car, bus, and truck stamps

Liquid or gel food colors

Plastic roller

Food color markers

Colored candy sticks

FONDANT PLAQUE FOR INSCRIPTION

4 ounces white fondant

Rolling pin

Cornstarch

Knife

Piping bag fitted with a #2 tip

Green piping gel

SHELL BORDER

White buttercream

Pastry bag fitted with a large star tip

PREPARATION TIMELINE

➡ **UP TO 2 WEEKS IN ADVANCE:**
Prepare the fondant boy on a truck

➡ **UP TO 1 WEEK IN ADVANCE:**
Prepare the fondant plaques

➡ **UP TO 3 DAYS IN ADVANCE OR DAY OF EVENT:**
Stamp the fondant plaques

➡ **UP TO 2 DAYS IN ADVANCE:**
Cover cake board in fondant if not using a cake plate

➡ **UP TO 2 DAYS IN ADVANCE:**
Bake cake

➡ **UP TO 2 DAYS IN ADVANCE:**
Fill and ice cake with buttercream

➡ **UP TO 1 DAY IN ADVANCE OR DAY OF EVENT:**
Decorate cake

John

CAKE ASSEMBLY

1. Begin by icing the cake with your choice of buttercream. The technique is the same as for masking a cake; however you will use more buttercream so that no parts of the cake can be seen. (See page 51–53 for icing techniques).

FINISHING

1. Make the modeled Boy on a Toy Truck for the cake topper (see page 103).
2. Cut out the plaques to the same dimensions as the sides of the cake.
3. Allow the plaques to dry on a parchment-lined baking sheet for 24 hours.
4. Spread a thin layer of liquid food color over a sheet of acetate or a piece of plastic wrap.
5. Roll a plastic roller in the food color and apply the color to the stamp.
6. Press the stamp onto the dried plaques.
7. Create background images on the plaques with the food color markers.
8. Allow the paintings to dry.
9. Gently place the finished plaques against the sides of the buttercream cake. The buttercream should hold the plaques in place, but if doesn't, apply a small amount of fresh buttercream to the backs of the plaques. Place the colored candy sticks at each corner of the cake.
10. Pipe the inscription directly on the plaque with the green piping gel.
11. Sprinkle the top of the cake with sanding surgar. Position the modeled figure and the plaque with the inscription atop the cake. Pipe small pearls of green piping gel randomly on the surface to look like clumps of grass.

VARIATIONS:

Different stamps can be used on the plaques to create an entirely different theme, such as holiday stamps, ballerina stamps, etc. Clay-modeling books have pictures and instructions for a wide variety of figures that could also be made out of fondant or gum paste.

OPPOSITE: *Stamping fondant plaques enables you to incorporate a theme into a cake and is a fun activity that even small children to participate in.*

MAKES 24 CUPCAKES

Embossed Monogram Cupcakes

PREPARATION TIMELINE

- **UP TO 1 WEEK IN ADVANCE:** Make the plaques
- **UP TO 1 DAY IN ADVANCE:** Bake the cupcakes
- **DAY OF EVENT:** Decorate the cupcakes

Components

Vanilla cupcakes

Embossed monogram plaques (see Embossed Monograms for Adult Cupcakes, page 137, for method)

Equipment and Materials

Blue buttercream

White nonpareils (see Shopping Resources, page 195)

1 pound pale blue fondant

Cornstarch

Rolling pin

Fluted oval cutter

Letter stamp or letter embossers

Parchment-lined baking sheet

Small offset palette knife

FINISHING

1. Make the plaques 24 hours before decorating.
2. Ice the cupcakes with the blue buttercream. The icing can be piped onto the cupcakes in a design or spread over the cupcakes with a small palette knife.
3. Pour the white nonpareils into a deep bowl and dip each cupcake, iced-side down, into the nonpareils.
4. Place the plaques either flat on top of each cupcake or stand them upright at an angle, as shown at right.

OPPOSITE: *Vanilla cupcakes with blue buttercream icing dipped in white nonpareils, with pale blue monogrammed plaques*

MAKES 24 CUPCAKES

Stamped Bugs and Flowers Cupcakes

PREPARATION TIMELINE

➡ **UP TO 1 WEEK IN ADVANCE:**
Prepare plaques

➡ **UP TO 1 DAY IN ADVANCE:**
Bake cupcakes

➡ **DAY OF EVENT:**
Decorate the cupcakes

Components

Cupcakes

Stamped fondant plaques (see Stamping Images on Fondant Plaques, page 163)

Equipment and Materials

Buttercream, ganache, or meringue for icing

Green nonpareils

8 ounces each yellow and white fondant

Oval and circle cutters

Rolling pin

Cornstarch

Parchment-lined baking sheet

Grasshopper stamp

Flower stamp

Green and orange food color

Plastic roller

Acetate sheet or an acetate page protector

METHOD

1. Lightly dust the work surface with cornstarch.

2. Roll out the yellow fondant to ⅛ inch thick and cut out the ovals with the oval cutter. Roll out the white fondant to ⅛ inch thick and cut out the circles with the circle cutter.

3. Allow the plaques to dry for 24 hours on a parchment-lined baking sheet.

4. Pour some dark green food color onto the acetate. Dip the roller in the color and apply the color to the grasshopper stamp.

5. Gently press the stamp onto one of the dried plaques. Repeat with the remaining plaques.

6. Pour some orange food color onto a clean piece of acetate. Dip the roller in the color and apply the color to the flower stamp.

7. Gently press the stamp onto one of the dried plaques. Repeat with the remaining plaques.

FINISHING

1. Pour the green nonpareils into a bowl. Dip each cupcake into the nonpareils, iced-side down, so that the icing is covered.

2. Insert a plaque into each cupcake so that they are standing straight up.

OPPOSITE: *Simple-to-make stamped flower and grasshopper plaques adorn these springtime cupcakes, which make a great decorating project to do with children.*

1635A
BURGUNDY
Wilton
BOURGOGNE

MAKES 24 CUPCAKES

Holiday Cupcakes

PREPARATION TIMELINE

➡ **UP TO 1 WEEK IN ADVANCE:**
Prepare stamped plaques

➡ **UP TO 1 DAY IN ADVANCE:**
Bake the cupcakes

➡ **DAY OF EVENT:**
Decorate the cupcakes

Components

Vanilla cupcakes

Buttercream, ganache, or meringue, or a combination of these, for icing

Holiday Plaques (see Pumpkin Plaques, Reindeer Plaques, and Chocolate Heart Plaques, pages 136–137, for the individual methods)

TO ASSEMBLE THE HOLIDAY CUPCAKES

1. Ice the cupcakes. The icing can be piped onto the cupcakes in a design or spread over the cupcakes with a small palette knife. For holiday cupcakes the icing can be colored to match the theme of the holiday, such as orange buttercream for Halloween.
2. Make the plaques and give them 24 hours to dry. Decorate the plaques.
3. Place a plaque on each cupcake.

OPPOSITE, TOP TO BOTTOM: *Pumpkin-shaped fondant plaques decorated with food color markers, heart-shaped chocolate plaques with piped chocolate inscriptions, and oval fondant plaques with stamped reindeer, all seated atop chocolate ganache-iced vanilla cupcakes*

Be Mine
Be Mine
Be Mine

APPENDIX A Scaling Recipes

SCALING RECIPES FOR DIFFERENT BATCH OR PAN SIZES

Depending on the cake you want to bake and the size of your gathering, you may need to convert a recipe for a cake, icing, or filling to accommodate a cake of greater or lesser size. Conversion to "scale" a recipe is a simple matter of multiplication. Follow these simple steps:

1. Select the recipe you want to convert.
2. Discern the *original yield* and your *desired yield.*
3. If both your *original yield* and *desired yield* are a pan size you will have to find the volume measure equivalent for each of these yields (see the chart Baking Pan Conversions and Equivalents, opposite).
4. Divide your *desired yield* by the *original yield* to find the *recipe conversion factor* or *RCF.*
5. Multiply the amount of each ingredient in your *original* recipe by the *recipe conversion factor.*
6. Use the new ingredient list resulting from step 5 to make the recipe for your *desired yield.*

For example, if you want to change a recipe for buttercream so that it makes 2 pounds (*desired yield*) rather than 1 pound (*original yield*): 2 pounds (*desired yield*) divided by 1 pound (*original yield*) = 2 (*recipe conversion factor*).

Or, if you want to make a 6-inch cake (*desired yield*) rather than an 8-inch cake (*original yield*), you need to use the volume of the pan to calculate (refer to the Baking Pan Conversions and Equivalents chart). 4 cups batter (*desired yield*) divided by 6 cups batter (*original yield*) = .666 (*recipe conversion factor*).

Once you figure out the recipe conversion factor, multiply the measurements for each ingredient by the recipe conversion factor. Sometimes you may need to round the result or convert it to a more logical unit of measure; 4 tablespoons, for example, is easier to measure as ¼ cup.

BAKING CONVERTED RECIPES

Remember to watch baking times carefully anytime you convert a recipe. If you have converted to a larger or smaller pan naturally the baking time will vary.

Shallower pans with the equivalent volume will have shorter baking times. If you substitute a pan that is shallower than the one specified in the recipe, reduce the baking time by 25 percent. If you substitute a pan that is deeper than the one specified in the recipe, increase the baking time by 25 percent.

Total volume refers to capacity of the pan when filled to the rim with water, not the volume of batter or dough that can be baked in the pan.

Although the sizes in this chart are considered standard, the actual size of your pan may vary slightly because different bakeware manufacturers may have slightly different specifications. To measure the dimensions of a pan, measure from inside edge to inside edge of the pan, ignoring any central tubes. To determine pan volume, measure the amount of water needed to fill the pan to the rim.

BAKING PAN CONVERSIONS AND EQUIVALENTS

Values for pan dimensions and total volume are approximate.

PAN SHAPE OR NAME	PAN DIMENSIONS	TOTAL VOLUME
Round cake pan	6 × 2 inches	4 cups
Round cake pan	8 × 1½ inches	4–5 cups
Round cake pan	8 × 2 inches	5–6 cups
Round cake pan	9 × 1½ inches	6 cups
Round cake pan	9 × 2 inches	7–8 cups
Round cake pan	10 × 2 inches	10–11 cups
Cupcake tin	2¾ × 1½ inches	½ cup
Heart-shaped cake pan	8 × 2½ inches	8 cups
Springform cake pan	8 × 3 inches	12 cups
Springform cake pan	9 × 2½ inches	12 cups
Springform cake pan	9 × 3 inches	13 cups
Springform cake pan	10 × 2½ inches	13 cups
Tube pan	7½ × 3 inches	6 cups
Tube pan	8 × 3 inches	9 cups
Tube pan	9 × 3 inches	12 cups
Tube pan	10 × 4 inches	16 cups
Bundt pan	7½ × 3 inches	6 cups
Bundt or fancy tube pan	9 × 3½ inches	9 cups
Angel cake pan	9 × 3½ inches	12 cups
Angel cake pan	10 × 4 inches	16 cups
Square cake pan	8 × 8 × 2 inches	8 cups
Square cake pan	9 × 9 × 1½ inches	8–9 cups
Square cake pan	9 × 9 × 2 inches	10 cups
Square cake pan	10 × 10 × 2 inches	12 cups
Rectangular cake pan	11 × 7 × 2 inches	6 cups
Rectangular cake pan	13 × 9 × 2 inches	8 cups
Pie pan	7 × 1¼ inches	2 cups
Pie pan	8 × 1½ inches	4 cups
Pie pan	9 × 1½ inches	5 cups
Pie pan	10 × 1½ inches	6 cups
Deep-dish pie pan	9 × 2 inches	6 cups
Deep-dish pie pan	10 × 2 inches	8 cups
Round tart pan	11 × 1 inches	4 cups
Quarter-sheet pan	13 × 9 × 2 inches	8 cups
Half-sheet pan	15 × 11 × 2 inches	14 cups
Loaf pan	8 × 4 × 2½ inches	5 cups
Loaf pan	8½ × 4½ × 2½ inches	6 cups
Loaf pan	9 × 5 × 3 inches	8–9 cups
Mini-muffin tin	1¾ × ¾ inches	2 tablespoons
Standard muffin tin	3 × 1¼ inches	½ cup plus 2 tablespoons
Extra-small soufflé dish	5 × 2 inches	1¼ cups
Small soufflé dish	5½ × 2½ inches	2½ cups
Medium soufflé dish	6¾ × 3 inches	6 cups
Large soufflé dish	7½ × 3½ inches	8 cups
Extra-large soufflé dish	8½ × 3¾ inches	8 cups
Charlotte mold	6 × 4¼ inches	7½ cups
Brioche mold	9½ × 3¼ inches	8 cups

APPENDIX B

Conversion Charts

TEMPERATURE CONVERSION

Degrees Farenheit and Celcius.

Values have been rounded.

32°F	0°C
40°F	4°C
140°F	60°C
150°F	65°C
160°F	70°C
170°F	75°C
212°F	100°C
275°F	135°C
300°F	150°C
325°F	165°C
350°F	175°C
375°F	190°C
400°F	205°C
425°F	220°C
450°F	230°C
475°F	245°C
500°F	260°C

WEIGHT MEASURES CONVERSION

U.S. and Metric. Values have been rounded.

¼ ounce	8 grams
½ ounce	15 grams
1 ounce	30 grams
4 ounces	115 grams
8 ounces (½ pound)	225 grams
16 ounces (1 pound)	450 grams
32 ounces (2 pounds)	900 grams
40 ounces (2¼ pounds)	1 kilogram

VOLUME MEASURES CONVERSION

U.S. and Metric. Values have been rounded.

1 teaspoon	5 milliliters
1 tablespoon	15 milliliters
1 fluid ounce (2 tablespoons)	30 milliliters
2 fluid ounces (¼ cup)	60 milliliters
8 fluid ounces (1 cup)	240 milliliters
16 fluid ounces (1 pint)	480 milliliters
32 fluid ounces (1 quart)	950 milliliters
128 fluid ounces (1 gallon)	3.75 liters

TO CONVERT OUNCES AND POUNDS TO GRAMS

Multiply ounces by 28.35 to determine grams; divide pounds by 2.2 to determine kilograms.

TO CONVERT GRAMS TO OUNCES OR POUNDS

Divide grams by 28.35 to determine ounces; divide grams by 453.59 to determine pounds.

TO CONVERT FLUID OUNCES TO MILLILITERS

Multiply fluid ounces by 29.58 to determine milliliters.

TO CONVERT MILLILITERS TO FLUID OUNCES

Divide milliliters by 29.58 to determine fluid ounces.

APPENDIX C Shopping Resources

J.B. PRINCE COMPANY
36 East 31st Street
New York, NY 10016-6821
PHONE: 800-473-0577
FAX: 212-683-4488
jbprince.com

KING ARTHUR FLOUR
The Baker's Store
135 Route 5 South
Norwich, VT 05055
PHONE: 802-649-3361
FAX: 802-649-3365
kingarthurflour.com

NEW YORK CAKE SUPPLIES
56 West 22nd Street
New York, NY 10010
PHONE: 212-675-2253 or 800-942-2539
FAX: 212-675-7099
nycake.com

PASTRY CHEF CENTRAL, INC.
1355 West Palmetto Park Road, Suite 302
Boca Raton, Fl 33486-3303
PHONE: 561-999-1282
FAX: 561-999-1282
EMAIL: customer_service@pastrychef.com
pastrychef.com

WILTON INDUSTRIES
2240 West 75th Street
Woodridge, IL 60517
PHONE: 630-963-1818 or 800-794-5866
FAX: 630-963-7196 or 888-824-9520
EMAIL: info@wilton.com
wilton.com

APPENDIX D

Templates

SIZES AND FUNCTIONS OF HEART-SHAPED CUTTERS

PIXIE WAVE

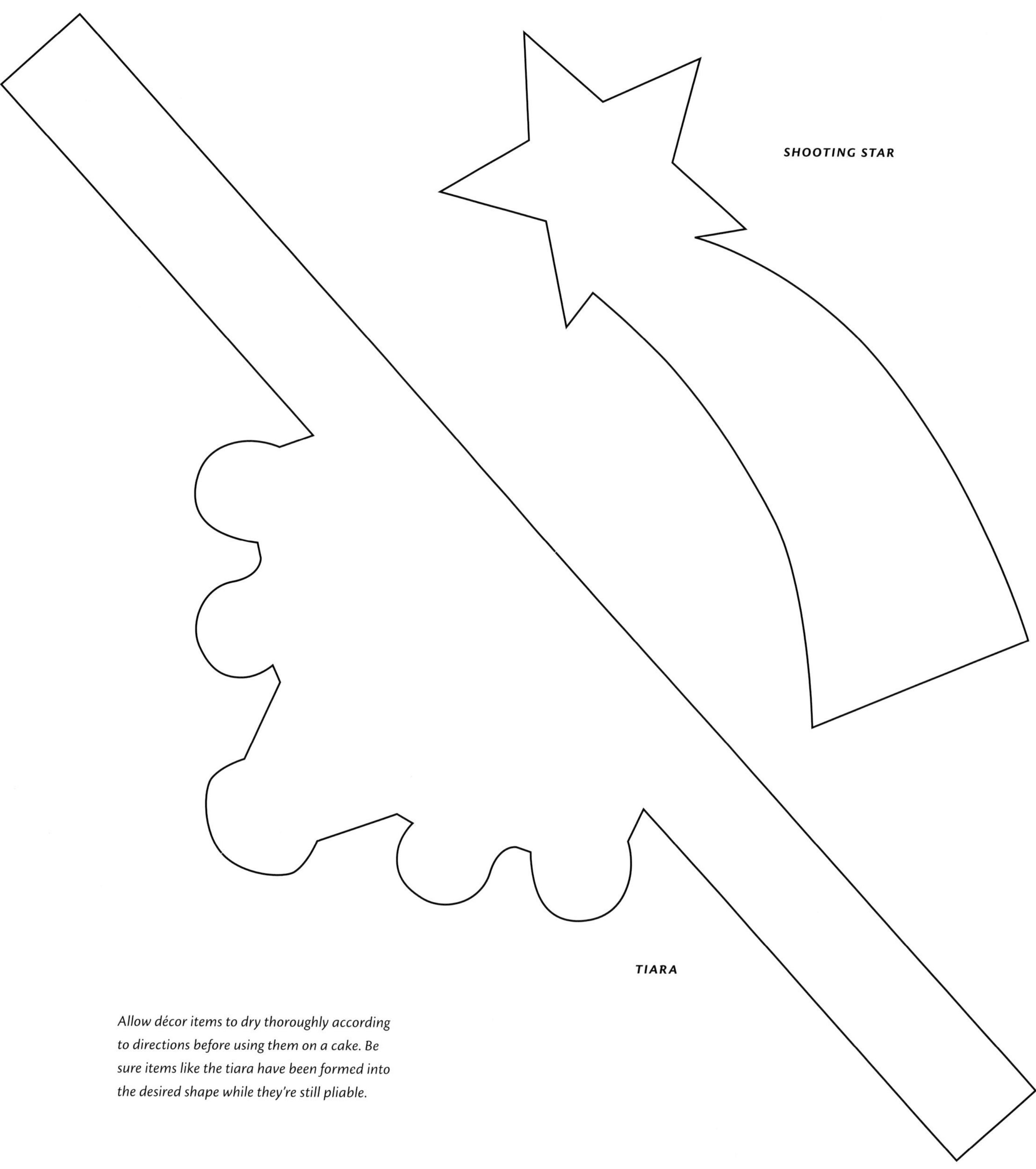

Allow décor items to dry thoroughly according to directions before using them on a cake. Be sure items like the tiara have been formed into the desired shape while they're still pliable.

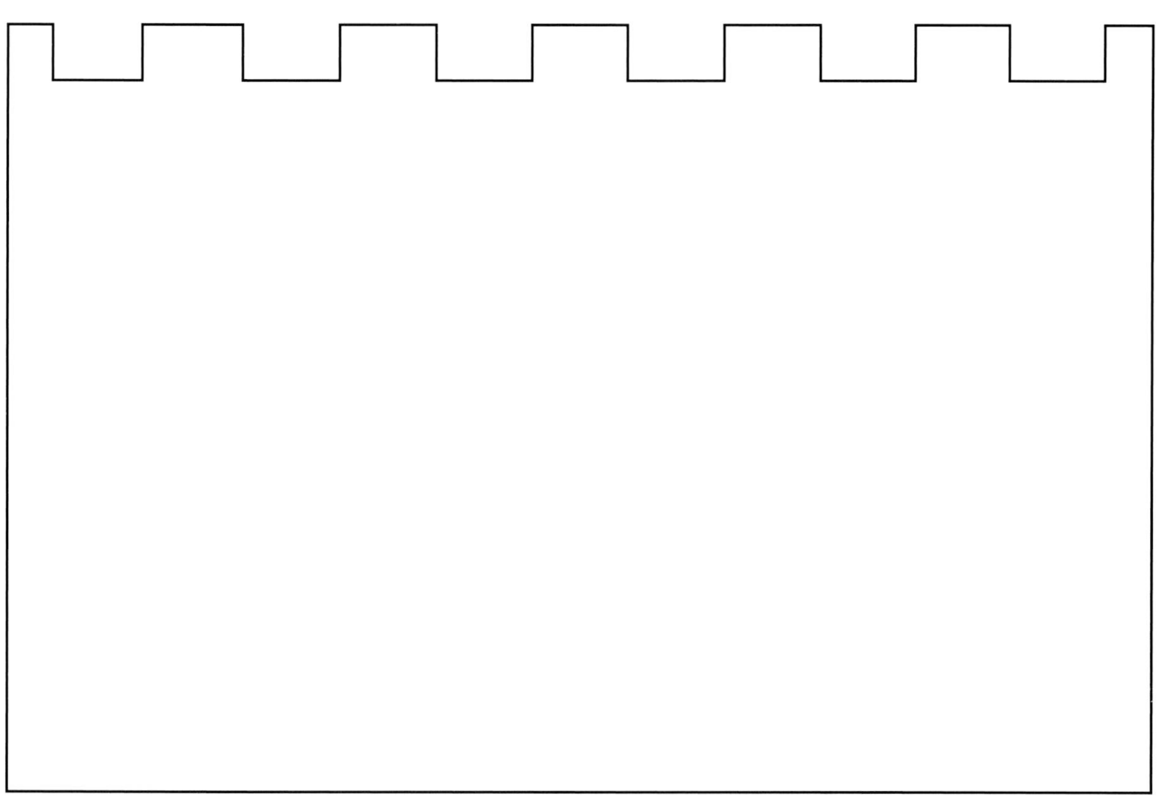

CASTLE WALL

MERMAID

MERMAID WAVE

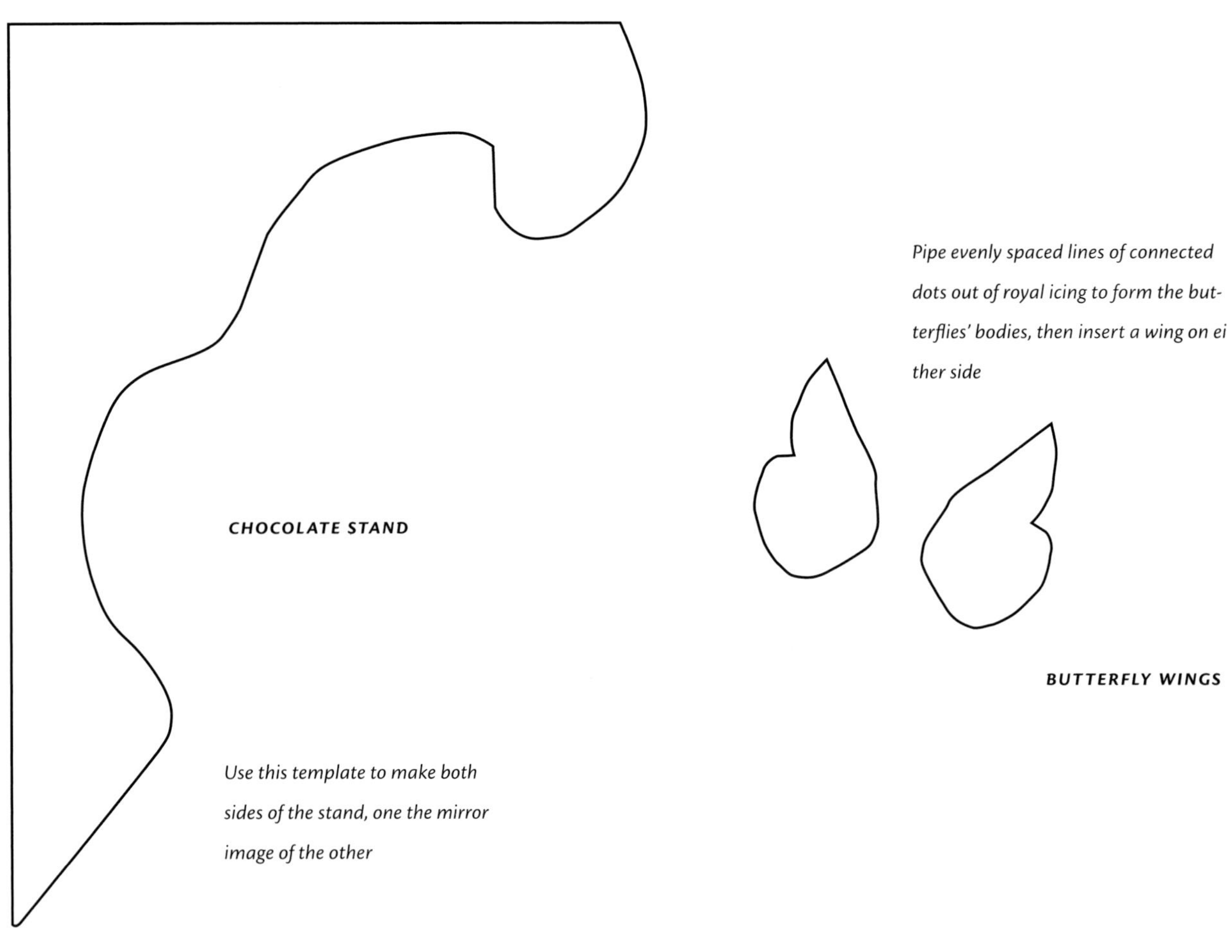

Pipe evenly spaced lines of connected dots out of royal icing to form the butterflies' bodies, then insert a wing on either side

Use this template to make both sides of the stand, one the mirror image of the other

Index

D

E

N

O

P

About the Authors and the Photographer

KATE CAVOTTI, C.M.B., C.H.E. is an associate professor in Baking and Pastry Arts at The Culinary Institute of America. She currently teaches Confectionery Art and Special Occasion Cakes. Her professional experience includes serving as Executive Pastry Chef at The Water Club in New York City and she is a Certified Master Baker.

ALISON MCLOUGHLIN, C.H.E. is an assistant professor in baking and pastry arts at The Culinary Institute of America. She currently teaches Basic and Classical Cakes. She is a 1993 honors graduate of The Culinary Institute of America and earned professional experience as owner/pastry chef at Pretty Cakes in Ridgefield, CT.

DIANE PADYS is a Seattle-based photographer whose work has appeared in a wide range of publications and advertising campaigns, and has garnered recognition including a World Image Award, a New York Art Directors Award, and an "Artist of the Year" award from *Vanity Fair* magazine.

ABOUT THE TYPE

The body text of this book is set in the OpenType version of Adobe Minion, an Adobe Originals typeface designed by Robert Slimbach for Adobe Systems in 1990. Heads, captions, and sidebar text are set in the same designer's Cronos. Both of these typefaces draw inspiration from the letterforms encountered in oldstyle types of the late-Renaissance.

Designed and composed by Kevin Hanek

Printed and bound in Singapore by Imago